C000145310

The Guide to the
HAP Standard

Humanitarian Accountability and Quality Management

HAP contact details and members

Contact details

HAP International
Maison Internationale de l'Environnement 2
Chemin Balexert 7–9
CH-1219 Châtelaine
Geneva, Switzerland
Tel: +41 22 788 1641
E-mail: secretariat@hapinternational.org
Website: www.hapinternational.org

HAP Members (at time of publication)

Australian Council for International Development; ACTED, CAFOD; CARE International; Christian Aid; Concern Worldwide, Danish Church Aid; Danish Refugee Council; Medical Aid for Palestinians; Medair; MERCY Malaysia; Norwegian Refugee Council; Office Africain pour le Développement et la Coopération; Oxfam GB; Save the Children UK; Tearfund UK; Women's Commission for Refugee Women and Children; World Vision International

Associate Members
DANIDA; DFID; MANGO; SIDA
[Note: these members are correct at time of publication]

Oxfam GB

Oxfam GB, founded in 1942, is a development, humanitarian, and campaigning agency dedicated to finding lasting solutions to poverty and suffering around the world. Oxfam believes that every human being is entitled to a life of dignity and opportunity, and it works with others worldwide to make this become a reality.

From its base in Oxford in the United Kingdom, Oxfam GB publishes and distributes a wide range of books and other resource materials for development and relief workers, researchers and campaigners, schools and colleges, and the general public, as part of its programme of advocacy, education, and communications.

Oxfam GB is a member of Oxfam International, a confederation of 13 agencies of diverse cultures and languages, which share a commitment to working for an end to injustice and poverty – both in long-term development work and at times of crisis.

For further information about Oxfam's publishing, and online ordering, visit

www.oxfam.org.uk/publications

For information about Oxfam's development, advocacy, and humanitarian relief work around the world, visit www.oxfam.org.uk

The Guide to the
HAP Standard

Humanitarian Accountability and Quality Management

First published by Oxfam GB for HAP International in 2008
Reprinted 2009

© HAP International 2008

The Guide to the HAP Standard: Humanitarian Accountability and Quality Management is published by Oxfam GB for HAP International as a contribution to improving humanitarian response. The views expressed are those of HAP International and are not necessarily endorsed by Oxfam GB.

ISBN 978-0-85598-600-1

A catalogue record for this publication is available from the British Library.

All rights reserved. Reproduction, copy, transmission, or translation of any part of this publication may be made only under the following conditions:

- with the prior written permission of the publisher; or
- with a licence from the Copyright Licensing Agency Ltd., 90 Tottenham Court Road, London W1P 9HE, UK, or from another national licensing agency; or
- for quotation in a review of the work; or
- under the terms set out below.

This publication is copyright, but may be reproduced by any method without fee for teaching purposes, but not for resale. Formal permission is required for all such uses, but normally will be granted immediately. For copying in any other circumstances, or for re-use in other publications, or for translation or adaptation, prior written permission must be obtained from the publisher, and a fee may be payable.

The information in this publication is correct at the time of going to press.

Published by Practical Action Publishing, Schumacher Centre for Technology and Development, Bourton on Dunsmore, Rugby, Warwickshire, CV23 9QZ, UK.
www.practicalactionpublishing.org

Since 1974, Practical Action Publishing (formerly Intermediate Technology Publications and ITDG Publishing) has published and disseminated books and information in support of international development work throughout the world. Practical Action Publishing Ltd (Company Reg. No. 1159018) is the wholly owned publishing company of Practical Action. Practical Action Publishing trades only in support of its parent charity objectives and any profits are covenanted back to Practical Action (Charity Reg. No. 247257, Group VAT Registration No. 880 9924 76).

Printed by Information Press, Eynsham.
Inners printed on recycled paper made from 100% post-consumer waste.
Cover printed on FSC-accredited 75% recycled paper.

Oxfam GB is a registered charity, no. 202 918, and is a member of Oxfam International.

Contents

What is this Guide for?

This Guide is a companion to the HAP Humanitarian Accountability and Quality Management Standard (2007), the full text of which is attached as Annex 1. The Guide follows the structure and format of the HAP Standard for ease of reference. It is aimed at the leaders, managers, and staff of humanitarian agencies that wish to improve the performance of their organisation, at those interested in assessing the case for seeking humanitarian quality assurance certification by HAP, and at those with responsibility for achieving compliance with the requirements of the HAP Standard. It will also be of relevance to individuals and organisations with a general interest in accountability. The Guide explains:

- The HAP Humanitarian Accountability and Quality Management Standard (2007)
- How agencies can meet the Standard
- How agencies can make an application for Certification
- How agencies will be assessed against the Standard in the HAP Certification process.

The Guide consists of the following parts:

Part I Introduction

The introduction explains how the HAP Standard and Certification scheme are new steps that both build upon and strengthen well-established and widely recognised good practices of humanitarian action. It discusses:

1. Accountability: 'the responsible use of power'

- Too many humanitarian standards?
- How were the HAP Standard and Certification system developed?
- HAP Standard: urgent corrective procedure.
- Survivors, beneficiaries, claimants, clients, or customers?

Part II Meeting the requirements of the HAP Standard

The first part of the Guide examines each component of the Standard, explains why it is important, how an organisation can meet these requirements, and how it will be measured in a Certification audit. It covers:

2. Qualifying norms for Certification

This chapter examines HAP's four 'qualifying norms', the prerequisites that an agency must meet before it can apply for HAP Certification. These are:

- A formal committment to humanitarian impartiality
- Not-for-profit status
- Demonstrated financial integrity
- A publicly available humanitarian accountability framework.

3. The Humanitarian Accountability Covenant

This section examines the Humanitarian Accountability Covenant, the part of the Standard that is concerned with practical challenges often experienced when putting humanitarian principles into practice. The four elements of the Covenant which merit further explanation and advice concerning compliance and assessment are:

- Principles for Humanitarian Action including non-compliance exoneration

- Declaration of additional interests
- Working with humanitarian partners.

4. Benchmarks for the HAP Standard

This section examines the six benchmarks that an agency must meet if it is to comply with the Standard and succeed in achieving Certification. Advice on 'good practice' to help agencies align their management systems to the Standard accompanies each benchmark. The six benchmarks cover:

- Humanitarian quality management systems
- Information provision to stakeholders
- Beneficiary participation and informed consent
- Staff competencies
- Complaints-handling mechanisms
- Learning and continual improvement.

Part III The HAP Certification Scheme

This part of the Guide explains what the Certification process is, how to make an application for Certification, what documents need to be submitted, and the likely resource requirements for meeting the Standard.

Annexes

1. Full text of the HAP Humanitarian Accountability and Quality Management Standard(2007)
2. Acronyms and glossary
3. Tools: a variety of practical tools for those wishing to enhance their management systems and bring them up to a level that meets the HAP Standard
4. Quality and accountability initiatives
5. Acknowledgements.

Supplementary information on the HAP website

Additional materials to be used in conjunction with the Guide and the Standard are available on the HAP website at: www.hapinternational.org.

The Guide itself is available from: www.oxfam.org.uk/publications.

Those seeking further guidance are welcome to write to the HAP Secretariat at: secretariat@hapinternational.org.

Part I: Introduction

1. Accountability: 'the responsible use of power'

I succeeded in getting together a certain number of women who helped as best they could to aid the wounded. It was not a matter of amputations or operations of any kind. But food, and above all drink, had to be taken around to men dying of hunger and thirst; then their wounds could be dressed and their bodies washed. ...

Oh, how valuable it would have been ... to have had a hundred experienced and qualified voluntary orderlies and nurses! ... As it was, there was no time for those who knew their business to give the needful advice and guidance, and most of those who brought their own goodwill to the task lacked the necessary knowledge and experience, so that their efforts were inadequate and often ineffective.

[Meanwhile] looters stole even from the dead, and did not always care if their poor wounded victims were still alive.

— Henri Dunant, 1859[1]

Whenever a [humanitarian] body is called upon to act or make a decision, it must first of all ask itself what the interests of the victims are, and if the action will serve those interests. This 'golden rule' will always enable the [agency] to solve most of the problems it encounters, with no danger of going wrong. In moments of difficulty, it will point the way more surely than the needle of a compass.

— Jean Pictet, 1979[2]

In 1859 a young Swiss traveller called Henri Dunant found himself caught up in the humanitarian tragedy that followed one of the most terrible battles of the nineteenth century.[3] While Dunant witnessed many extraordinary acts of kindness amidst the harrowing scenes he so vividly described, the founder of modern humanitarianism also made two profound observations. First, the ever-present risk that ill-directed compassion can do more harm than good. Second, that traumatic events are inherently disempowering, exposing all those affected to opportunistic and sometimes extreme forms of exploitation.

While Dunant recorded these observations nearly 150 years ago, he might equally have been describing a contemporary disaster relief operation. The joint evaluations of the international responses to the 1994 genocide in Rwanda and the 2004 Indian Ocean tsunami both drew attention to the harmful and wasteful consequences of humanitarian action launched without adequate consultation with the people affected by the disaster. So why, after 150 years of institutionalised humanitarian assistance, should there be so many emergency relief programmes that fail to live up to Jean Pictet's[4] 'golden rule'?

In every humanitarian transaction there is an imbalance of circumstantial power between those able to give help and those in urgent need of assistance. This inequality between provider and receiver means that the act of giving is often exercised without the consent of the person in need.

When compared with the wider community of professions dedicated to improving human welfare, the scope for emergency relief workers to misuse or abuse their power is perhaps exceptional. While many public services are governed by professional associations that define standards, set entry qualifications, and deal with allegations of professional negligence and misconduct in order to protect the lay public, humanitarian work has generally been practised outside the scope of such regulatory systems.

It would clearly be wrong to insist that all acts of human compassion be administered by 'licensed humanitarians', but in the absence of such controls the humanitarian community is consequently largely self-selected, with no mandatory qualifications for either individuals or organisations engaging in emergency relief work. Furthermore, as a great many humanitarian disasters occur in situations where administrative systems are weak, contested, or compromised by the crisis itself, the humanitarian giver–receiver relationship is often conducted in a state of virtual judicial impunity. Relief agencies usually work under no immediate political or legal obligation to gain the consent of persons affected by disasters, or to offer complaints-handling and redress mechanisms to correct mistakes and compensate people unintentionally harmed by the emergency response.

However, through observing basic ethical safeguards and applying relevant management and technical skills, it is possible to assure the quality of humanitarian work, and to ensure that the power of the humanitarian giver is neither misused nor abused.

The Humanitarian Accountability Partnership (HAP) defines accountability as 'the responsible use of power'. The body was founded in 2003 to promote the HAP Principles of Accountability – seven basic rules that together can ensure the responsible use of humanitarian power. In 2007 HAP released its Standard in Humanitarian Accountability and Quality Management, against which it is now possible to assess compliance with proven good practice in humanitarian work. The Standard is a rigorously researched and tested product that identifies six practical 'benchmarks' for effective humanitarian quality management. Each benchmark has been selected because disaster survivors, in dialogue with the humanitarian community, have confirmed that the prescribed practice is necessary for achieving the best possible humanitarian results in an accountable and affordable manner.

As a consequence, agencies that attain compliance with the HAP Standard will raise the quality, impact, and efficiency of their humanitarian work, protect the dignity of those affected by disasters, and improve the security, job satisfaction, and reputation of participating humanitarian aid workers.

HAP is founded upon the belief that such accomplishments deserve wider recognition, and the HAP Certification Scheme has been developed to serve this objective. Subject to a thorough independent analysis of an organisation's management system, HAP Certification can be conferred upon an agency that has proved that it can be relied upon to deliver quality humanitarian work wherever circumstances allow.

This Guide is designed to provide practical advice for the leaders, managers, and staff of organisations which want to comply with the HAP Standard and to enjoy recognition of this achievement through attaining HAP Certification.

Too many humanitarian standards?

HAP is not the first inter-agency initiative to seek to address the observed shortcomings of the humanitarian aid system. These go back at least as far as Henri Dunant himself and the founding of the Red Cross movement. The *Code of Conduct for the International Red Cross Movement and NGOs in Disaster Relief* and The Sphere Project's *Humanitarian Charter and Minimum Standards in Disaster Response* have further elaborated the ethical and technical frameworks for humanitarian response. People In Aid, the Active Learning Network for Accountability and Performance (ALNAP), and the Compas Qualité of Groupe URD and Coordination Sud have designed systems, codes, and tools for improving human resource management, monitoring and evaluation, and programme quality management respectively. So, in a field where some argue that there are already more than enough standards, codes, and principles, was it really necessary for HAP to create its own Accountability and Quality Management Standard?

5

The answer to this question lies in HAP's basic purpose as a voluntary international regulatory body devoted to promoting humanitarian accountability. When HAP was mandated in 2003 by its founders to 'monitor and report on the implementation of HAP International's Principles of Accountability and to accredit its members accordingly', it was apparent that it could not do this in a fair and affordable manner using any of the existing codes, standards, or tools. This was simply because none of the existing tools had been designed to verify compliance with HAP's Principles of Accountability.

Furthermore, while other inter-agency initiatives have made important contributions to the identification and promotion of good humanitarian practices, these have not necessarily been developed to fulfill all the criteria required for inclusion in the HAP Standard, namely mission-criticality, affordability, and measurability.

How were the HAP Standard and Certification Scheme developed?

HAP initiated the development of its Accountability and Quality Management Standard in 2005, using a consensus-building process that placed great emphasis on consulting all interested parties. A stakeholder analysis was carried out and a reference group was established, comprised of representatives of disaster-affected people, NGOs, various humanitarian quality and accountability initiatives, United Nations agencies, government donors, host authorities, and other interested individuals. The development of the HAP Standard followed the International Organization for Standardization's Directives on *Rules for the Structure and Drafting of International Standards*, ensuring that all interested parties in the humanitarian community were consulted. The process was divided into three main stages:

- A broad consultation with key stakeholders took place between July 2005 and December 2006. The reference group provided feedback on each draft and regional consultations were held in Bangladesh, Kenya, and the UK. The Standard was field-tested in three countries using three very different agencies.[5]

- The Editorial Steering Committee met and finalised the draft Standard in December 2006 and, with a few changes, the Standard was formally adopted by the HAP Board in January 2007.

- Finally, certification trials were conducted with MERCY Malaysia in Kuala Lumpur and with the Danish Refugee Council in Copenhagen, to fine-tune the Certification process and the audit guidelines. A group of independent auditors was selected, and trained to carry out baseline analyses and Certification audits from early 2007.

The principle of continual improvement applies as much to the ongoing development of the HAP Standard as it does to agencies that comply with it. In this respect, learning about humanitarian accountability and quality management continues, and it is expected that a revised HAP Standard will be released in 2009, taking account of lessons learned during the application of the 2007 version.

HAP Standard: urgent corrective procedure

Although there is an ongoing process of continual review of the Standard, there is also a mechanism that can be invoked for urgent review and correction. Where there is firm evidence or plausible grounds for believing that compliance with any element of the HAP Standard will compromise the safety or well-being of disaster survivors, agency staff, or third parties, the HAP Secretariat should be notified immediately.

Agencies and individuals should send details of the circumstances of the case to: secretariat@hapinternational.org or to the Executive Director of HAP (e-mail address available at: www.hapinternational. org). To enable the matter to be reviewed quickly, please provide the following information:

- Identify the component of the Standard that is causing concern (e.g. the qualifying norms, the Principles for Humanitarian Action, working with partners, Benchmarks 1–6, their related requirements, or means of verification).
- Identify who may be adversely affected by the application of this element of the Standard.
- Explain why, how, and when they may be affected, giving as much detail as possible.
- If possible, recommend specific changes (additions, deletions, or modifications) to the text of the Standard that would resolve the problem identified.

On receipt of such information, the Secretariat will review the case, notify the HAP Board accordingly and, if necessary, issue a corrective to the Standard and distribute an urgent advisory notice to HAP members, Certification applicants, and other interested parties.

Nomenclature: beneficiaries or survivors?

While setting up HAP and then developing the Standard, there was much debate about terminology, especially with regard to terms used to describe persons of concern to humanitarian agencies. Throughout this text, the phrase 'disaster survivors' is used to refer to all living persons who have been directly affected by armed conflict or by other calamitous events such as tsunamis, earthquakes, and famines. The term 'beneficiary' refers only to persons who have been designated as the intended recipients of humanitarian assistance or protection. In this Guide, the term 'beneficiary' is concerned with the transactional relationship between the agency and the persons to whom the agency has given an undertaking of assistance.

HAP intends no value judgement about either the aid provider or the aid recipient when using the term 'beneficiary', and indeed is sympathetic to the view that other terms such as 'claimant', 'customer', or 'client' may be more appropriate with regard to acknowledging the dignity and rights of disaster survivors. However, 'beneficiary' is used throughout HAP's founding Statute and it appears no less than six times in the HAP Principles of Accountability. To drop the term altogether would serve little useful purpose, while potentially giving the misleading impression that HAP has changed its focus or mandate – which is certainly not the case.

It needs emphasising that beneficiaries should never be viewed, addressed, or assisted as a homogenous group, with a fixed universal culture that either cannot or should not change. Beneficiary groups contain the same diversity and complexity of social, cultural, gender, and political differentiation as any other group of individuals, and good humanitarian management practices will recognise and engage with this at all stages of the project cycle. For example, in assessing needs, the disaggregation of those affected by a disaster will highlight diverse needs and capacities in relation to women, girls, men and boys, separated children, elderly people, people with disabilities, and other minority or potentially marginalised groups.

Field practitioners and policy makers are equally responsible for ensuring that humanitarian action is designed as far as is practically possible to meet the specific assistance and protection needs of individual disaster survivors, rather than some sort of generalised and abstract beneficiary.

Notes

1 H. Dunant (1986) *A Memory of Solferino*, ICRC: Geneva.
2 J. Pictet (1979) 'The Fundamental Principles of the Red Cross – Commentary', ICRC: Geneva.
3 Henri Dunant (1828–1910) estimated that 80,000 combatants died from wounds, infections, and epidemics following the battle of Solferino. His first-hand memoir inspired the founding of the Red Cross Movement.

4   Jean Pictet (1914–2002) was Director-General of the International Committee of the Red Cross and the lead author of the Fundamental Principles of the Red Cross.

5   World Vision International in Sri Lanka, OFADEC in Senegal, and the Danish Refugee Council in Somalia.

Part II: Meeting the requirements of the HAP Standard

2. Qualifying norms for Certification

The qualifying norms are four important criteria that agencies must meet before they can apply for HAP Certification. They are: humanitarian impartiality, not-for-profit status, financial account-ability, and a publicly available humanitarian accountability framework. An agency that submits an application for Certification will need to demonstrate that it fulfils these qualifying norms (see Annex 1, The HAP Standard 1.3). Each of these is examined below in greater detail.

Qualifying norm 1: Impartiality

Committed to provide humanitarian assistance on an impartial basis.

1. What does impartiality mean?

HAP's principles for humanitarian work are derived mainly from the Fundamental Principles of the Red Cross movement, proclaimed in Vienna in 1965 and the result of a century of work in humanitarian crises. These principles affirm the essential importance of 'humanity', i.e. the belief that all human beings have an inalienable and equal right to live in dignity. Humanitarianism is thus concerned with the prevention and alleviation of human suffering, wherever it occurs, and the right of all persons to receive and give assistance.

Impartiality means providing humanitarian assistance in proportion to need and with respect to urgency, and without discrimination based on gender, age, race, impairment, ethnicity, or nationality, or because of political, religious, cultural, or organisational affiliation. In other words, there should be no social, political, cultural, or religious bias or prejudice in the delivery of aid.

2. Why is impartiality important?

While everyone has an equal moral right to humanitarian assistance, an impartial assessment of needs will invariably identify individuals or groups of people with different survival requirements. Humanitarian agencies must always try to act in an impartial manner so that those most in need are helped first. To achieve this, it is necessary to disaggregate affected populations to ensure that people who are often overlooked or discriminated against (e.g. elderly people, women, children, people with disabilities, minorities) are properly considered when deciding who has the most pressing need for assistance.

However, as political interest in humanitarian aid has grown, the possibilities of its use for political or military purposes have also increased. A military-led protection project intended to win hearts and minds, or relief intended to compensate for the adverse consequences of political loyalty, are unlikely to be consistent with the principle of humanitarian impartiality. Therefore the integration of humanitarian assistance into wider political or military strategy threatens the impartiality of the system for humanitarian aid resource allocation and delivery. In turn, the safety of humanitarian workers is undermined when their actions are not perceived to be impartial.

Because emergency aid that is provided on an impartial basis is the most effective way of saving and protecting lives, the HAP Standard requires that all applicants for Certification have a prior commitment to the principle of impartiality.

3. How will this requirement be assessed?

At the application stage an agency must provide evidence that it is committed to the principle of humanitarian impartiality. This may be found in the organisation's statutes, constitution, charter, or mandate. If no such reference exists, the governing body of the agency will have to make a formal declaration of its commitment to humanitarian impartiality. This could also be incorporated into the agency's humanitarian accountability framework – see qualifying norm 4 below.

Qualifying norm 2: Not-for-profit status

Formally declared as a not-for-profit organisation in the country or countries where it is legally registered and where it conducts humanitarian work.

1. What is a not-for-profit organisation?

A not-for-profit organisation is one that is established for charitable, humanitarian, or educational purposes and which has no intent to make profits from its programme for its staff, members, or any other shareholders/stakeholders. The not-for-profit principle is comparable with the Red Cross principle of 'voluntary service', or selflessness. Jean Pictet wrote: *'In speaking of selflessness, we mean that [the agency] has no interests of its own, or at least that its interests coincide with those of the persons it protects or assists.'* [1] A not-for-profit humanitarian agency is concerned only with the humanitarian interests of the persons who require help. Many countries set their own detailed criteria for what is meant by 'not-for-profit', which must be met by organisations wishing to operate on their territory.

2. Why is it important to be a not-for-profit organisation?

A humanitarian organisation, by definition, exists first and foremost to address the suffering of crisis-affected populations. To focus on profits or on political objectives would compromise the ability of an organisation to give assistance in an impartial and humane manner, as its decisions would be affected by its own need to achieve commercial, political, or military goals. Although the profit motive is said to generate efficiency, it is also clear that the humanitarian motive opens doors and attracts voluntary financial and moral support in a manner seldom rivalled by commercial or military organisations. A not-for-profit status may also confer preferential benefits such as tax exemptions, work permits, and other privileges, all of which can confer significant comparative advantages upon not-for-profit agencies.

3. How will this requirement be assessed?

At the application stage, an agency must provide evidence of its registration as a not-for-profit body in its 'home' country and a formal declaration of not-for-profit status in the countries where it conducts humanitarian activities. This will require submission of relevant registration documents given by government authorities, annual accounts, or in exceptional circumstances where no such documents exist, a signed statement by the agency's governing body confirming its not-for-profit status.

Qualifying norm 3: Financial accountability

Complies with the requirements for financial accountability under the law in the country or countries where it is legally registered and where it conducts humanitarian work.

1. What are the financial accountability requirements?

An agency that wishes to achieve compliance with the HAP Standard must be in good financial standing. This is defined as meeting the legal requirements for financial accountability in its country of registration or incorporation, and in the countries where it conducts operations.

2. Why is financial accountability important?

Being accountable is intrinsically linked with being responsible for the efficient and effective use of the resources donated to and managed by the agency. However, in the final analysis, disaster-affected populations bear the true costs of mismanagement, negligence, or corruption. So while it is important for donors, it is genuinely vital for disaster survivors that an agency is accountable for all of its assets.

3. How will this requirement be assessed?

At the application stage, the agency must submit:

- A statement that it meets the legal financial accountability requirements in its 'home' country of incorporation or registration. This information may be found in annual reports or audits.

- Independently audited accounts for the three previous years and, where possible, the current expenditure plan. Independent financial auditing provides some level of guarantee against fraud and misuse of funds, and would be a minimum requirement for HAP to consider Certification.

- A list of current humanitarian programmes (see example in Table 1 below) to enable HAP to understand the size, scale, capacity, and timeframe of programmes in which the agency is engaged.

17

Table 1: Sample list showing all active operations, with start and end dates and volume indicators

Country Include all programmes in country	Start	End	Partners Name humanitarian implementing partners	Beneficiaries	Staff	Comments Donors, evaluations, audits etc.
South Sudan	24.02.95	Open				
WatSan project in Bor County	01.01.07	31.12.07		10,000	47	
Health programme in Upper Nile	01.05.06	30.09.07		54,000	115	

© HAP International

Qualifying norm 4: Humanitarian accountability framework

Makes a publicly available statement of its humanitarian accountability framework.

1. What is a humanitarian accountability framework?

HAP defines a humanitarian accountability framework as 'a set of definitions, procedures, and standards that specify how an agency will ensure accountability to its stakeholders. It includes a statement of commitments, a baseline analysis of compliance, and an implementation policy, strategy, or plan'. In short, a humanitarian accountability framework consists of a list of the minimum standards that an agency commits to meeting in its humanitarian work, an implementation plan for achieving these, and an explanation of the means available for stakeholders to hold it to account for these. A branding or marketing strategy is not the same as a humanitarian accountability framework, although it should not be inconsistent with it.

2. Why is a humanitarian accountability framework important?

Stakeholders, whether they are staff, volunteers, customers, clients, intended beneficiaries, or donors, usually like to know what an agency 'stands for', what it really believes in, what it considers to matter most when deciding what to do, and how it intends to go about doing it. Answers to these questions are often critical factors for people making a choice about which agency to work for, or which agency to donate to. For people in a crisis, there is an even more crucial concern: can the agency be relied upon to fulfil its pledges? If not, then time spent queuing to register for assistance might be better spent on other survival activities – this is a choice that may literally be a matter of life or death.

A humanitarian accountability framework therefore helps all stakeholders to make better-informed decisions, with more predictable and more desired results. In humanitarian crises, predictability is crucial for enhancing inter-agency co-ordination and improving overall humanitarian outcomes. This is why donors are increasingly favouring the use of 'framework partnerships', and also emphasising the need for a publicly available accountability framework.

3. What should be included in a humanitarian accountability framework?

The humanitarian accountability framework is perhaps the least familiar to aid practitioners of the four qualifying norms set out in the HAP Standard and, as a required component of the HAP Certification application, its preparation may at first sight appear to be a daunting task. However, in practice it should be a straightforward exercise. In the first instance, it is concerned only with identifying and, where appropriate, clarifying the status of, existing commitments made by the agency.

In some cases, particularly with small or new agencies, there may be very few formal commitments in place, either internally developed ones or commitments adopted from external standard-setting bodies. For agencies such as these, links on the HAP website can be used to build up a menu of the better-known humanitarian standards currently on offer. For larger and longer-established agencies, the problem is more likely to be a multitude of commitments, several of which may overlap, some of which may be out of date, and others which may be irrelevant to humanitarian work.

In developing a humanitarian accountability framework, the following guidance may be considered when deciding what should be included or excluded:

- **Relevance:** A humanitarian accountability framework should include only those commitments that are demonstrably linked to the quality and accountability of the agency's own humanitarian programme. For example, a specialised medical agency would not be advised to make commitments regarding civil engineering standards, and vice versa.

- **Concreteness:** To be useful, an accountability framework should include only commitments that can be verified or measured by tangible indicators. This does not exclude the use of qualitative concepts such as 'dignity' or 'well-being', but it does require the identification of an affordable and routinely employed means of monitoring these, such as contact group interviews or opinion surveys.

- **Realism:** The standards to which an agency subscribes should be achievable under 'normal' circumstances, i.e. within the competencies and capacity that the agency is usually able to deploy, and which are appropriate to the typical humanitarian context. A humanitarian accountability framework is therefore more likely to include a commitment to minimum standards and less likely to make pledges to deliver state-of-the-art excellence.

- **Attribution:** While humanitarian agencies collectively seek to improve the well-being of those affected by disaster, a humanitarian accountability framework should focus upon verifying the application of established good practices by the agency itself and not upon factors over which it has no control or little influence. However, this does not mean that the framework should only cover internal management processes. For example, it could include co-ordination norms such as the InterAction Field Cooperation Protocol, consultation norms of the kind contained in the Sphere common standards, or advocacy norms such as those set out in the IANGO Charter.

- **Coherence:** Overall, a humanitarian accountability framework should be internally consistent. A lack of coherence might result from the following:

    o **Ambiguous codes, standards, or principles:** A humanitarian accountability framework should provide guidance on what can be expected of an agency, and what will be done if it fails to meet these expectations. However, some of the humanitarian community's codes, standards, and principles have not been developed for the purpose of accountability, and they sometimes therefore lack measurable indicators or a consideration of their affordability. Some are written in a purely aspirational mood, with the required commitment defined by imprecise verbs such as 'strive', 'endeavour', or 'attempt'. When the commitment does not specify how hard the agency should strive or endeavour, there is great scope for interpretation, negotiation, and resulting incoherence.

o **Overlap:** Standards often cover similar ground but use different definitions, benchmarks, or indicators. For example, staff competencies are referred to in the People in Aid Code, the Compas Qualité, the Sphere common standards, and the HAP Standard. The participation of beneficiaries is referred to in the Compas Qualité, the Red Cross/NGO Code of Conduct, Sphere, and HAP. Before making a commitment to any of these, the agency should itself assess whether different standards are complementary, and which can be included in its framework without creating incoherence.

o **Lack of prioritisation:** The ability to meet commitments is invariably dependent upon a combination of leadership, availability of human and financial resources, and the presence of a conducive environment. Sometimes, even when leadership and context are favourable, a lack of resources may force a difficult choice between quality and quantity objectives, even though meeting both is considered vital for the survival of those affected. In such circumstances, a simple list of commitments does not help in deciding between options. In this sort of situation the humanitarian accountability framework should provide guidance, either by ranking the commitments in order of importance or by setting out a process for dealing with such difficult choices. A simple way to rank an agency's commitments is to identify which are obligatory, which are formal guidelines, and which are simply aspirational. If the status of a commitment is unclear, the answers to the following three questions may help to ascertain its standing in the organisation:

- At what level in the organisation was it adopted or endorsed? This should indicate its **formal** status.

- Is it monitored and, if so, how is this done? This may demonstrate its **observed** status.

- What are the repercussions for non-compliance? This may reveal its **actual** standing.

Ideally, the formal, observed, and actual status of a commitment should be consistent. Indications that a commitment is not observed should not automatically lead to a conclusion that it ought to be. Rather, it indicates that its status should be reviewed and clarified by the appropriate authority in an organisation.

The humanitarian accountability framework should always be seen as work in progress. It is a document that should be updated often, as an agency clarifies and improves its quality and accountability systems. The humanitarian accountability framework that an agency produces at the very beginning of its journey towards full Certification, when it is making a baseline analysis of compliance and an improvement plan, will almost certainly be different from the framework it submits when it is ready for Certification.

4. How will this requirement be assessed?

At the application stage, the HAP requirement is that a 'publicly available' statement of an agency's humanitarian accountability framework be submitted. 'Publicly available' means accessible to the public, including intended beneficiaries and humanitarian partners, e.g. through the Internet, in printed or audiovisual information materials, or on public notice-boards. The HAP Standard ultimately requires that the humanitarian accountability framework is available in 'languages, formats, and media that are accessible and comprehensible for beneficiaries and specified stakeholders'.

At a minimum, on first application, the agency must submit a statement summarising its humanitarian accountability framework and detailing the following:

Statement of commitments

- List of all standards, codes, guidelines, mandate, principles, charter, etc. to which an agency has committed itself and which are evidently relevant to the quality of its humanitarian programme. These may be internally generated by the agency itself, or developed for collective use by a group of agencies or by a standards-setting body. Standards for collective use might include, for example, the *International Red Cross Movement and NGO Code of Conduct in Disaster Relief;* The Sphere Project's *Humanitarian Charter and Minimum Standards in Disaster Response;* Coordination Sud's *Compas Qualité,* the People In Aid *Code of Good Practice;* InterAction's *PVO Standards,* ACFID's *Code of Conduct;* or the Secretary-General's *Bulletin on Special Measures for Protection from Sexual Exploitation and Abuse.*

- For agencies seeking HAP Certification, commitment to the principles for humanitarian action set out in the HAP Humanitarian Covenant are obligatory.

Baseline analysis

- In order to be able to monitor progress, an agency needs to establish a starting point or current status assessment. This is an essential management tool that allows an agency to identify gaps, strengths, and weaknesses in relation to its accountability and quality management commitments. It will also identify those commitments that the agency is occasionally or consistently unable to meet. Improvement plans can then be drafted to address gaps identified.

- A baseline analysis must be carried out by agencies seeking to be certified against the HAP Standard.

- The baseline analysis may be carried out by the agency itself or by an independent body. In either case, the process should be conducted in a manner that is comparable with the HAP

Certification audit process, as described in Part III of the Guide.

Implementation policy, strategy, or plan

* Once an agency's commitments have been identified and gaps in compliance have been assessed, a quality and accountability standards implementation plan can be developed. This should explain the management arrangements, procedures, and processes that are in place, or will be put in place, to turn the agency's commitments into a reality on the ground. It will include a method of monitoring progress to ensure that the agency is constantly moving forward, and that it is quality-assured. For example, the implementation plan might include:
  ○ SMART[2] objectives: building from the baseline analysis, what actions are needed to move towards full compliance?
  ○ Progress indicators: which indicators will be chosen and how will these be monitored and reported upon?
  ○ Designation of management responsibilities: who has overall responsibility for the implementation of each specified quality or accountability commitment?
  ○ Stakeholder communication plan: who needs to know about the commitment and how will they get to know about it?
  ○ Staff competencies: who needs to be skilled in the application of the specified commitment and how will these competencies be acquired?
  ○ Knowledge management: how are good practices identified and disseminated?
  ○ Complaints-handling: how are complaints concerning quality compliance issues addressed in a safe, consistent, and fair manner?
  ○ Improvement plans: how will the implementation plan and the performance of the staff involved be monitored and evaluated?

5. Will everything in the humanitarian accountability framework be assessed?

HAP Certification is concerned primarily with how an agency complies with the HAP Standard. However, as the humanitarian accountability framework may also make reference to other standards, codes, principles, or policies, the question arises of whether HAP will also assess compliance with these commitments. The answer is broadly 'no', although the HAP assessment will seek to ascertain the following:

- Has the agency been definitive and comprehensive in listing those commitments and declaring those interests that are evidently relevant to the quality of its humanitarian programme?

- Has the agency carried out a baseline analysis against all of its commitments?

- Has the agency prepared an implementation plan, strategy, or policy, and defined progress indicators to measure its performance in implementing these commitments?

Apart from where there are coincidental overlaps, a HAP audit will not attempt to assess compliance with other standards, codes, or principles in the rigorous manner that it will audit compliance with the HAP Standard, given that:

- HAP is not the intellectual owner of these other standards and it has no mandate to assess compliance with them.

- HAP may not have the technical knowledge to assess compliance with them.

- The additional complexity and costs of auditing other standards, codes, or principles may be prohibitive.

6. Example of a humanitarian accountability framework pro-forma

A humanitarian accountability framework can take many forms. Most crucially, it must suit the organisation that it is designed for, specifically with regard to the use of specialist language and the names and related acronyms given to specific posts, work groups, policies, and management processes familiar to the agency. However, it must also be made available in versions that are accessible and comprehensible to stakeholders or their designated representatives. The example given in Table 2 shows how an agency's commitments might be mapped, as the first step in developing a humanitarian accountability framework.

Table 2: Example of a pro-forma for a humanitarian accountability framework

Quality and accountability commitments			Baseline analysis		
Commitments	Authority	Obligation	Implementation mechanism	Partner status	Compliance status
Mandate/ charter	Board	Binding	Strategic plan – emergency	Guideline	
Programme quality policy	Programme department	Binding	Quality management system – programme department workplan – emergency response section Budget – adequate	Compliant	
Red Cross/ NGO Code of Conduct	Unknown	Guideline	None	N/A	
Sphere Humanitarian Charter and Minimum Standards	Executive director	Guideline	None	Mixed	
HAP Standard	Executive director	Binding	Humanitarian accountability workplan	Mixed	
People in Aid Code	Human resources director	Binding	Departmental workplan	Good	
Field Co-operation Protocol	Emergencies director	Guideline	None	Unknown	

© *HAP International*

28

Implementation plan

SMART objective	Progress indicator	Action
Review corporate quality policy		
Update and streamline quality management system		
		Clarify status with IFRC. Review by Programme Department
		Review by Board and, if adopted, include in programme quality policy and implement through quality management system
		Review by Board and, if adopted, include in programme quality policy and implement through quality management system
		Include in Programme Department quality management system
		Clarify status with InterAction

3. The Humanitarian Accountability Covenant

The part of the Standard referred to as the Humanitarian Accountability Covenant includes a common set of principles to which agencies seeking HAP Certification must commit. These Principles for Humanitarian Action provide a common practical definition of humanitarianism for agencies seeking to achieve compliance with the HAP Standard. More importantly, they offer a framework that can help to guide and adapt humanitarian action in a consistent and accountable way to the realities of challenging operational environments and when working with humanitarian partners. This section of the Guide examines three elements of the Humanitarian Accountability Covenant:

- The HAP Principles for Humanitarian Action
- Declaration of additional interests
- Working with humanitarian partners.

The HAP Principles for Humanitarian Action

1. What are the HAP Principles for Humanitarian Action?

In designing the HAP Standard, it was necessary to adopt a clear definition of what being 'humanitarian' entails for organisations seeking to comply with it. The International Committee of the Red Cross is rightly seen as the guardian of the spirit and law of humanitarianism, and the HAP Principles for Humanitarian Action owe a large debt to the accumulated wisdom contained in the 1965 Fundamental Principles of the Red Cross.[3]

However, the Fundamental Principles contain three 'organic principles' that are specific to the Red Cross movement and which are not necessarily relevant to other humanitarian organisations; furthermore, they do not explicitly address the question of accountability. The HAP Principles for Humanitarian Action therefore exclude two of the Red Cross organic principles (unity and universality), while adding five accountability-related principles (informed consent, duty of care, witness, transparency, and complementarity). The third Red Cross organic principle – voluntary service – is effectively contained within HAP's 'not-for-profit' qualifying norm.

2. Why are the principles important?

Humanitarian crises are typically complex and fluid. They affect individuals and groups whose needs also change over time in different ways. Of necessity, humanitarian agencies have recognised the need for great flexibility in applying policy principles within diverse and sometimes hostile environments. The medical practice of ranking the order in which emergency patients are treated (known as *triage*), exemplifies how humanitarian organisations can be forced to select the 'least worst' option from within a range of 'bad choices'. Providing humanitarian aid often requires prioritisation of objectives, e.g. in response to issues of relative need, urgency, available resources, access, protection, staff security, and so on. This happens each time humanitarian needs outstrip response capacities, creating dilemmas with which humanitarian agencies are all too familiar.

It was in recognition of the challenge posed by such situations that the International Committee of the Red Cross ranked the Fundamental Principles, thereby creating a guidance tool when confronting hard choices. As Jean Pictet's celebrated commentary on the Red Cross Principles states: *'The principles do not all have the same importance. They have a hierarchical order, indicated at the outset by the sequence in which they are presented in the Proclamation ... The ICRC is obliged to interpret these principles with a certain degree of flexibility, taking into account the particular circumstances in each individual case.'* [4]

The HAP Humanitarian Covenant similarly acknowledges that the contexts in which humanitarian agencies operate can impose constraints beyond the control or influence of the agency, and that these in turn demand operational compromises. In reality there will be occasions when one or more benchmarks in the Standard cannot or should not be fully met, for justifiable reasons. The Humanitarian Covenant groups the Principles for Humanitarian Action into primary, secondary, and tertiary levels. [5]

While the HAP Standard expects a compliant agency to commit to all the principles with equal determination, real circumstances may still force an agency to compromise on a tertiary principle, such as neutrality, in order that it is allowed to run an operation that can fulfil a secondary or primary principle, such as meeting humanitarian needs in an impartial way. For example, many NGOs are obliged to pay taxes to warring parties before they are allowed to operate, in effect compromising on a strict interpretation of neutrality, in order that they can deliver life-saving aid. In such cases, exoneration for non-compliance would be granted under the HAP Covenant.

3. How will compliance with the Principles for Humanitarian Action be assessed?

The HAP Certification process does not audit compliance with the Principles for Humanitarian Action, because to do so would be too complex and costly, and of questionable benefit. Several of the principles are philosophical in nature, and verification of compliance would be subject to insoluble debates about interpretation and attribution. In contrast, a HAP Certification audit is focused upon verifiable indicators, including the requirement that an agency must have a humanitarian accountability framework.

However, because difficult operating environments will sometimes legitimately justify non-compliance with the HAP benchmarks, it is necessary to have a transparent and consistent way in which exoneration for non-compliance can be granted when justified. In this respect, the proper question should be: how will cases of non-compliance with the benchmarks be exonerated? The answer is that claims of 'justifiable non-compliance' will be analysed and assessed by reference to the HAP Principles for Humanitarian Action.

4. When will exoneration be granted?

The HAP Certification process allows the certification auditor to recommend 'exoneration' whenever reasonable justification is given. It is impossible to explain all of the specific cases in which exoneration might be granted because of the enormous number of variations that exist in humanitarian operating environments. Instead, Table 3 reproduces the Principles for Humanitarian Action from the HAP Standard in the left-hand column, and in the right-hand column provides a few simple examples of cases where exoneration may be granted.

Table 3: Examples of exoneration cases

Principles	Notes and examples of context-specific constraints
Primary principles:	Exoneration may be justified only where humanitarian action is prevented by factors beyond the control or influence of the agency.
Humanity *Upholding the right of all persons to receive and give assistance*	• Exoneration for non-compliance with the 'humanitarian imperative' (the primary principle of humanity) may be justified only when an agency either lacks the ways (permissions or partners) or means (resources) to intervene effectively.
Impartiality *Providing humanitarian assistance in proportion to need and with respect to urgency, without discrimination based upon gender, age, race, impairment, ethnicity, and nationality or by political, religious, cultural, or organisational affiliation*	• In cases of extreme urgency or insecurity, or as a result of the policies and practices of donors or host authorities, impartiality may be unavoidably compromised. • **Urgency:** It would be inappropriate to conduct a detailed survey of the needs of flood victims before undertaking urgent search-and-rescue operations. • **Access:** When relief supplies can only be delivered by air-drop it may be possible to make only approximate considerations regarding specific gender, age, and disability data (although consultation with people familiar with the affected population and relevant demographic records may enable these to be quite accurate). • A failure to assess needs in relation to gender, disability, and age that are entirely due to shortcomings within the agency cannot be exonerated.
Secondary principles:	Exoneration must be justified by reference to the primary principles.
Informed consent *Ensuring that the intended beneficiaries, or their representatives, understand and agree with the proposed humanitarian action and its implications*	• In cases of urgency or insecurity it may not be possible to secure the informed consent of beneficiaries, but the 'humanitarian imperative' may still justify intervention – e.g. airdrops of relief supplies to flood victims. • Where cholera is endemic, the treatment of drinking water supplies might be justified by the primary principles prior to gaining informed consent. • Where government policies prevent meaningful consultation with affected people, an intervention may still be justified by the primary principles, although those most familiar with the affected population (e.g. a diaspora) may provide a reliable 'proxy' reference group.

Principles	Notes and examples of context-specific constraints
Duty of care *Ensuring that humanitarian assistance meets or exceeds recognised minimum standards pertaining to the well-being of the intended beneficiaries*	• In cases where host authorities have set standards below the level of internationally recognised disaster relief norms (e.g. shelter specifications, drugs policies) the agency may be obliged to comply with these on the grounds that the only alternative is to breach the primary principles by doing nothing. • In cases where recognised minimum standards can only be met by the arbitrary selection of a few beneficiaries, an agency may be exonerated for deciding to provide a smaller ration than recommended in order to comply with the principle of impartiality.
Witness *Reporting on policies or practices that affect the well-being of disaster survivors*	• If reporting human rights abuses might result in the closure of an effective relief programme, the agency may be exonerated for giving the primary principles precedence over the duty to bear witness, although in most cases it is possible to pass on information to others who are in a position to use it. • In cases where the safety and security of disaster survivors or field staff might be compromised by the publication of information about the disaster-affected population, exoneration for non-disclosure would be justified when this was necessary to protect an ongoing humanitarian effort.
Tertiary principles:	**Exoneration must be justified by reference to the primary or secondary principles.**
Transparency *Ensuring that all relevant information is communicated to intended beneficiaries or their representatives, and other specified parties*	• In cases where the publication of beneficiary lists and entitlements might compromise their security (i.e. primary principles) or their privacy (i.e. secondary principles), non-disclosure would be justified.
Independence *Acting under the authority of the governing body of the agency and in pursuit of the agency's mandate*	• Agencies often cede a degree of their sovereign independence when they enter funding contracts, partnership agreements, or registration mechanisms. Such compromises can be justified provided that these can be demonstrated to enable an agency's capacity to further the primary and secondary principles.

Principles	Notes and examples of context-specific constraints
Neutrality *Refraining from giving material or political support to parties to an armed conflict*	• In some conflict zones, working in certain areas may prevent an agency from working in other areas because an authority forbids it from working on both sides of a conflict. While this does not prevent the agency from acting impartially in its area of operation, it may adversely affect perceptions of its neutral status. • Agencies are sometimes obliged to choose between absenting themselves from a disaster zone or paying taxes or 'tithes' to authorities closely linked to warring parties, in order to gain permission to carry out humanitarian work. • Assessing 'net humanitarian benefit' in both cases cited above is extremely complicated, but this kind of analysis would be necessary before exoneration could be considered.
Complementarity *Operating as a responsible member of the humanitarian assistance community*	• It may sometimes be deemed necessary to work outside the parameters set by national or international co-ordination bodies in order that the agency can comply with the primary and secondary humanitarian principles.

© HAP International

As the examples above demonstrate, an exoneration scheme is both necessary and complex. The guidance given to HAP's auditors is to approach the question of exoneration with an open mind, recognising that humanitarian work will often present agencies with difficult choices and occasional moral dilemmas, in situations where information is scarce and often unreliable. The Principles for Humanitarian Action provoked more debate than any other element of the HAP Standard during the drafting process. In recognition of this, HAP is committed to further learning from evidence and common sense, and will not promote a dogmatic interpretation of the Principles for Humanitarian Action in the Certification scheme.

Declaration of additional interests

1. What are 'additional interests'?

The HAP Standard requires that agencies seeking Certification declare 'additional affiliations, interests, values, and policies where these may have a direct bearing upon the well-being of disaster survivors, intended beneficiaries, and other specified stakeholders'.

The word 'additional' means commitments that go beyond the substance and scope of the HAP Principles of Accountability and the HAP Principles for Humanitarian Action. Because on its own this is a very open-ended requirement, the conditional phrase 'having a direct bearing upon' needs to be emphasised. The HAP Standard (see Benchmark 2) requires that information about the agency that beneficiaries and other stakeholders should be aware of is readily available. However, it is for the agency, in consultation with its stakeholders, to decide what this means in practice. HAP's concern is mainly to know that it has been done.

The 'declaration of additional interests' should be included in the inventory of commitments made in an agency's humanitarian accountability framework, and in most cases it will not be necessary to prepare a separate document.

2. Why declare additional interests?

The purpose of the declaration of additional interests is to encourage a 'no surprises' approach, giving all stakeholders the opportunity to better understand the nature of the agency and to ensure greater predictability in, and understanding of, its relevant affiliations, policies, partnerships, and relationships.

3. What should be included in a declaration of interests?

It would be impossible to produce a list of all the additional interests that humanitarian agencies have that could be defined as being of direct relevance to the well-being of disaster survivors, intended beneficiaries, and other stakeholders. Instead, a simple classification of the kinds of interests that may be relevant is provided in Table 4, with some examples given for illustrative purposes only.

Table 4: Examples of 'additional interests'

	Type	Examples
Affiliation	National, regional, and global networks	ACBAR and ANCB (Afghanistan), Coordination Sud (France), InterAction (USA), ACFID (Australia), Philippines Council for NGO Certification, DENIVA (Uganda), DEC (UK), Bond (UK), Asian Disaster and Response Network, SCHR, VOICE (EU), ICVA
	Professional, technical, or thematic networks	ALNAP, People in Aid, Sphere, Inter Agency Working Group, ECB
	Partnerships and federations	CARE International, Oxfam International, World Vision International, Caritas Internationalis, Lutheran World Federation, Plan International, MSF International, International Federation of Red Cross and Red Crescent Societies
	Operational arrangements	Operation Lifeline Sudan, UN Water and Sanitation cluster
Interests	Client group focus	Women (e.g. Women's Commission on Women Refugees and Children), children (e.g. Save the Children), elderly people (e.g. Help the Aged), people with disabilities (e.g. Action on Disability and Development), refugees (e.g. Refugees International)
	Technical or functional focus	Water (e.g. WaterAid), health (e.g. Médecins du Monde), animal health (e.g. Vétérinaires Sans Frontières)
Values and policies	Values	Religion (e.g. Islamic Relief, Christian Aid), human rights (e.g. Human Rights Watch)
	Policies	Red Cross Movement and NGO Code of Conduct in Disaster Relief, People in Aid Code, Do No Harm, ACFID Code of Conduct

© *HAP International*

4. How will the declaration of additional interests be assessed?

The declaration of additional interests will not be 'assessed' in the Certification audit because there is no related benchmark or compliance indicator for this declaration included in the Standard. However, an agency must document and publish its humanitarian accountability framework (to meet qualifying norm 4 and Benchmarks 1 and 2), and an agency's 'additional interests', as defined above, should be included in this document.

Working with humanitarian partners

1. What is a 'humanitarian partnership'?

The first people to provide humanitarian assistance are invariably neighbours, local community-based organisations, local NGOs, and government organisations. The Red Cross/NGO Code of Conduct states: '*We shall attempt to build disaster response on local capacities.*' Humanitarian aid agencies work within complex networks of contractual relationships involving donors, suppliers, official regulatory or licensing bodies, outsourced sub-contractors, and many others who help and occasionally hinder their work. However, the term 'partner' is often reserved for those bodies with the most direct relationship with disaster survivors and beneficiaries, and which are often referred to as 'implementing partners'.

The HAP Standard defines humanitarian partnership as 'a relationship of mutual respect between autonomous organisations that is founded upon a common purpose with defined expectations and responsibilities. Partnerships can be established with or without formal contractual agreements. Partners can be small, community-based organisations or large national or international institutions. A **humanitarian partnership** is one in which two or more bodies agree to combine their resources to provide essential goods or services for disaster survivors.'

2. Why are humanitarian partnerships important?

According to HAP Accountability Principle 7 (see Annex 1, The HAP Standard), 'Members are committed to the implementation of these principles if and when working through implementation partners'. However, many agencies have expressed the view that the phrase 'working through' implies a relationship of subservience on the part of implementing partners. The HAP Standard was therefore developed within a new consensus that places greater emphasis upon the ideas of complementarity and mutuality as key principles for defining 'quality' in humanitarian partnerships. In particular, the idea of imposing standards or principles upon humanitarian partners was rejected in favour of an approach that emphasises common objectives, trust, mutual respect, and negotiation over differences. However, there was also consensus about the need to establish a 'bottom-line' understanding about basic values that must exist for a partnership to flourish. The HAP Standard therefore requires that certified agencies will at a minimum:

- explain their accountability and quality management obligations as HAP Standard bearers to their humanitarian partners;
- seek ways and means to improve the quality of the partnership with respect to the Principles of Accountability and the Principles for Humanitarian Action.

3. How will this requirement be assessed?

The HAP auditing process will first ascertain if an agency seeking Certification has explained its accountability and quality management obligations to its humanitarian partners. Second, the audit will examine how the requirement to improve the quality of partnership is being pursued.

The audit will pay special attention to how an agency is enabling its humanitarian partners to become compliant with the Principles of Accountability and the Principles for Humanitarian Action. Generally speaking, the methods used for assessing compliance by the applicant agency will include:

- Interviews with one or more of the agency's humanitarian partners, selected at random, to assess their knowledge and experience of the agency's humanitarian accountability framework, partnership improvement strategy, and complaints-handling mechanism.

- A review of documents, e.g. improvement plans for partners; monitoring and evaluation reports; contracts with partners showing that relevant support is built in; records of consultation with partners about setting up complaints-handling procedures (minutes of meetings; contractual inclusion); written copies of complaints-handling procedures; sample complaints, etc.

- Interviews and focus group discussions with beneficiaries during field visits to verify that the complaints-handling procedures are working.

More information on improving and assessing 'quality partnerships' is provided in the section explaining the benchmarks below.

4. Benchmarks for the HAP Standard

An agency that wishes to comply with the HAP Standard must first fulfil the qualifying norms and then meet the Benchmarks and their related requirements. HAP Certification can be granted when an independent auditor confirms that an agency complies with the means of verification specified in the Standard. The HAP Standard has six benchmarks. These are reproduced in the exact words contained in the Standard in the box on the facing page.

In this section of the Guide, each Benchmark is examined in turn, using the following format:

1. What does the Benchmark mean?
2. Why it is important?
3. How will it be assessed?
4. Suggestions for good practice.
5. References to further tools and information.

HAP Humanitarian Accountability
and Quality Management Standard (2007)

The Six Benchmarks

1. The agency shall establish a humanitarian quality management system.

2. The agency shall make the following information publicly available to intended beneficiaries, disaster-affected communities, agency staff, and other specified stakeholders: (a) organisational background; (b) humanitarian accountability framework; (c) humanitarian plan; (d) progress reports; and e) complaints-handling procedures.

3. The agency shall enable beneficiaries and their representatives to participate in programme decisions and seek their informed consent.

4. The agency shall determine the competencies, attitudes, and development needs of staff required to implement its humanitarian quality management system.

5. The agency shall establish and implement complaints-handling procedures that are effective, accessible, and safe for intended beneficiaries, disaster-affected communities, agency staff, humanitarian partners, and other specified bodies.

6. The agency shall establish a process of continual improvement for its humanitarian accountability framework and humanitarian quality management system.

Links with the humanitarian accountability framework

Throughout this section, numerous references are made to the humanitarian accountability framework, which is described in Chapter 2: Qualifying norms for Certification. While drafting the Standard, there was much debate about whether the humanitarian accountability framework should be designated as a Benchmark or as a qualifying norm. However, this mattered primarily with regard to the logic and convenience of its placement in the text of the Standard, because in either case there was a general consensus that the Standard had to make the formulation of a humanitarian accountability framework compulsory. After much discussion, the humanitarian accountability framework was finally designated as a qualifying norm. Nevertheless, it is also explicitly referred to in:

- Benchmark 1 in relation to its implementation through a quality management system
- Benchmark 2 in relation to its public availability
- Benchmark 4 in relation to staff competencies
- Benchmark 5 in relation to complaints-handling
- Benchmark 6 in relation to continual improvement.

In this respect, the humanitarian accountability framework is a unifying tool that is an integral part of the Standard and an essential component of the Benchmarks.

Benchmark 1: Humanitarian quality management system

The agency shall establish a humanitarian quality management system.

1.1 The agency shall document its humanitarian accountability framework referring to all relevant internal and external accountability and quality standards, codes, guidelines, and principles committed to by the agency.

1.2 The agency shall demonstrate that its humanitarian quality management system enables implementation of its humanitarian accountability framework.

1. What is a 'humanitarian quality management system'?

Quality in a product or service is not what the supplier puts in. It is what the customer gets out and is willing to pay for. A product is not quality because it is hard to make and costs a lot of money, as manufacturers typically believe. This is incompetence. Customers pay only for what is of use to them and gives them value. Nothing else constitutes quality.

— Peter Drucker, management writer[6]

The HAP Standard takes it that a humanitarian agency's principal 'customers' are disaster survivors, who are meant to benefit from the agency's humanitarian programme. While those most adversely affected are not usually required to pay for the assistance that is offered, disaster survivors are always expected to devote time and due attention to the receipt, consumption, and utilisation of assistance. But because their continued existence itself is at stake, the participation of disaster survivors should never be taken for granted.

Although images of disaster 'victims' all too often show people apparently doing nothing but waiting for help to arrive, in reality survivors are almost always engaged in a desperate struggle to stay healthy and alive. For them, each moment counts in how it can be

45

used to improve the prospects for, and quality of, survival – for themselves and for their family, their neighbours, and their community. Therefore, when offering assistance, humanitarian agencies ought to have verified that their intended beneficiaries do value what is on offer, and that survivors are not wasting vital time and energy on what may be more 'photo opportunity' than rigorous assessment or distribution.

Thus, Peter Drucker's formulation of what constitutes quality could be paraphrased for humanitarian agencies as follows: disaster survivors appreciate only what is of use to them and gives them value. Nothing else constitutes humanitarian quality.

The HAP Standard therefore defines a **humanitarian quality management system** as a 'designated set of processes that enable continual improvement in an agency's performance in meeting the essential needs and respecting the dignity of disaster survivors'. A humanitarian quality management system is, in essence, the means by which an agency's humanitarian accountability framework is implemented, monitored, and improved over time.

The quality management system comprises the resources that the agency uses to meet its quality and accountability objectives, while the framework describes its essential quality and accountability objectives, stating who is responsible and where, when, and how each commitment will be met and progress measured.

In some agencies a humanitarian accountability framework will be part of a more comprehensive accountability framework that provides a publicly available statement about all of the agency's key corporate or organisational commitments. Similarly, its humanitarian quality management system may be an element in its overall corporate or organisational quality management system.

Benchmark 1 requires that an agency prepares a humanitarian accountability framework (as explained in Chapter 2 under the qualifying norms) and puts this into practice through its quality management system. The implementation plan or strategy included in the framework should cover every aspect of the 'plan–do–check–act' quality assurance cycle (see Annex 3, Tool 6: Plan–do–check–act). It should:

- identify stakeholders
- state their needs and expectations
- outline relevant 'quality' commitments
- contain SMART objectives and progress indicators
- designate management responsibilities
- designate human, financial, and logistical resources
- outline partnership strategies
- identify staff development plans
- specify a knowledge management strategy that includes monitoring, evaluation, learning, and improvement objectives.

2. Why is Benchmark 1 important?

The humanitarian sector has developed many standards and guidelines, but fewer means of verifying their implementation. Humanitarian standards often remain aspirational, due to weaknesses in quality management practices. A humanitarian quality management system can address these shortcomings through:

- empowering beneficiaries and other stakeholders
- fostering a culture of accountability and learning
- streamlining internal and external communications
- clarifying priorities and development needs for staff.

In turn, an effective humanitarian quality management system will:

- yield better humanitarian outcomes
- improve overall efficiency
- improve staff motivation and retention
- enhance consent and improve agency security
- strengthen the agency's organisational profile and fundraising performance.

3. How will this benchmark be assessed?

The means of verification for this Benchmark are set out in the Standard itself as follows.

Benchmark requirements	Means of verification
1.1 The agency shall document its humanitarian accountability framework referring to all relevant internal and external accountability and quality standards, codes, guidelines, and principles committed to by the agency.	1 Review copy of documented humanitarian accountability framework and cross-reference with all relevant agency commitments including the agency's non-disclosure policy. 2 Verify that the document is made publicly accessible throughout the agency and to its humanitarian partners. 3 Review agency's strategy to support humanitarian partners in developing their capacity to comply with the Principles of Accountability and Principles for Humanitarian Action.
1.2 The agency shall demonstrate that its humanitarian quality management system enables implementation of its humanitarian accountability framework.	1 Confirm existence of and review implementation procedures for the humanitarian quality management system. 2 Interview humanitarian partners to confirm awareness of agency's humanitarian accountability framework.

Working with partners

An agency working with humanitarian partners is required to:

- ensure that its partners are aware of, and understand, the agency's humanitarian accountability framework
- show that it has a strategy for supporting and strengthening the capacity of its partners to apply the HAP Principles of Accountability and Principles for Humanitarian Action (the guidance on good practices below gives further advice on what such a strategy should contain).

4. Suggestions for good practice

This section gives some suggestions about how to develop a humanitarian quality management system and a humanitarian accountability framework. Most organisations will already have systems and documentation policies in place, so this may be best treated as a checklist, although HAP does not claim that it is definitive or applicable to all organisations.

Step 1: Make quality an organisational goal

- Secure a definitive statement about quality and accountability by the highest authority in the agency. This can help to ensure that 'quality and accountability' are embedded in an agency's standard operating procedures. The process of doing this may also help to clarify an agency's priorities and what it can, and cannot, commit to.
- Ensure that the agency's board is committed and that its CEO has overall responsibility.

Step 2: Define stakeholders

- Define who the agency's stakeholders are.
- Clarify how their needs and expectations are defined in terms of quality and accountability.
- Clarify how the agency's stakeholders are consulted or represented. This may raise very important questions

concerning the agency's governance (see Annex 3, Tool 8: Community engagement tools: stakeholder analysis).

Step 3: Make a list of 'quality' commitments

An agency's commitments should be relevant to its own stakeholders and in particular to its primary 'customers', its programme beneficiaries.

- Review the agency's organisational mission and/or mandate and identify all relevant established 'corporate' quality and accountability commitments.

- Review and record all relevant commitments made at head office level.

- Review and record all relevant commitments made at field level.

- Agree indicators for all relevant commitments (the list of commitments should be documented in the agency's humanitarian accountability framework).

Step 4: Carry out a baseline analysis

- Evaluate where the agency currently stands in relation to the commitments made, using the indicators developed. Involving staff and stakeholders at different levels can enhance this process.

- Identify gaps in compliance, and set a timeline and an improvement plan for addressing these gaps (the baseline analysis should be documented in the agency's humanitarian accountability framework.)

Step 5: Improve the humanitarian quality management system

Identify the systems, mechanisms, processes, and resources that are currently being used, and what is now needed for implementation. Systems might include operations, logistics, financial, human resources, marketing/fundraising, policy, and learning. In each, clarify:

- **Management responsibilities**
  - Assign responsibility for implementation.
  - Create specialised posts to enable implementation if required.
  - Include reference to the HAP Standard in job descriptions, work plans, and targets.
  - Ensure that responsible staff can integrate the relevant elements of the quality and accountability commitments into their work.
  - Ensure that all staff who need to know about the HAP Standard do know through induction, refresher training, and information handouts, newsletters, etc.
  - Make knowledge and delivery of the HAP Standard part of the performance appraisal process.

- **Knowledge management procedures**
  - Include the HAP Standard in key organisational materials such as strategy papers, operations manuals, training materials, etc.
  - Include the HAP Standard at all stages of programme design, implementation, and evaluation.
  - Consider how the HAP Standard can apply to different programmes, projects, countries, and contexts.
  - Make the HAP Standard visible in the workplace.

- **Budget arrangements**
  - Ensure that implementation of the HAP Standard is budgeted for, whether under a single budget-holder or decentralised to all relevant budget-holders.

- **Monitoring and evaluation procedures**
  - Put in place processes to ensure that the implementation plan is functioning, and that it is monitored and continually improved.

- **Documentation**
  - ° Clarify what documentation is required for the quality management system, and establish who produces it, who revises it, who uses it, who retains it, and what restrictions apply to its distribution.

Step 6: Monitor and evaluate

Institute a monitoring process to check how accountability and quality assurance commitments are being met. This will require setting up systems and processes for monitoring, indicators for measuring progress, and procedures for capturing lessons learned and feeding them back into the system. Verification of implementation in the following dimensions should be covered:

- **Management responsibilities:** organisational structure; job descriptions; interviews with staff (varying levels, roles, locations, etc.).

- **Staff:** training manuals (induction and refresher); staff handouts; job descriptions, workplans, appraisal reports; visibility of Standard in workplace; interviews with staff.

- **Knowledge management:** key organisational documents for references; field visits; interviews with beneficiaries.

- **Budgets:** budget allocations.

- **Partners:** partner assessment and feedback.

- **Monitoring and evaluation:** monitoring and evaluation reports. Monitoring needs to take place at two levels: (1) monitoring whether the quality management system is working; (2) monitoring whether the 'quality and accountability' commitments are being met. Commitments (e.g. gender policy) will require different indicators (e.g. targets for female staff, inclusion of female beneficiaries in community committees) from those used to measure the actual system.

Step 7: Continually improve

- Capture feedback and lessons learned for improving the process in line with HAP Benchmark 6.
- Ensure that new standards and good practices in the humanitarian sector are reviewed and incorporated as appropriate.

Step 8: Partnership arrangements

The strategy for working with humanitarian partners should include the following:

- **Partner selection:** Ensure that there is a sound and equitable selection process which provides equal opportunities for women's groups and other marginalised communities.

- **Contractual agreements:** Include commitments by the agency to the partner and vice versa. An undertaking to implement accountability principles can be included in the contract itself or made on a more informal basis.

- **Capacity building:** Assess the partners' strengths and weaknesses in relation to the HAP Principles of Accountability and Principles for Humanitarian Action and develop a plan for improvement and training. An improvement plan should include a baseline analysis (partners' current status, strengths, and weaknesses in relation to the different aspects of the Principles); identification of areas of potential improvement, listed in order of prioritisation; identification of resources, noting what it would take to support and improve the partner in each area identified; timeframe (planning deadlines and support in a realistic and affordable way); indicators (draft clear and attainable indicators for progress, including those relating to gender mainstreaming and child protection); and a joint agreement to be drawn up between the partner and the agency to work together on the implementation of this plan.

- **Information:** Keep partners informed about the accountability and quality commitments made by the agency.

- **Technical support:** Make arrangements to provide support as and when required.

- **Continual improvement:** Ensure that monitoring and evaluation are essential parts of programmes implemented by partners, to enable continual learning.

- **Complaints-handling:** Procedures for handling complaints should be set up. These include procedures implemented by the partner to enable beneficiaries to complain to the partner and to the agency directly, as well as procedures for the partner and the agency to complain or give feedback to one another (the implementation system should be documented in the agency's humanitarian accountability framework).

5. References to further tools and information

See the following Tools in Annex 3 for further assistance:

- Tool 6: Plan–do–check–act quality assurance cycle (PDCA).
- Tool 8: Community engagement tools: stakeholder analysis

For further guidance on quality standards and quality management systems, see the ISO 9000 Council website at: www.iso9000council.org/index.htm

Benchmark 2: Information

The agency shall make the following information publicly available to intended beneficiaries, disaster-affected communities, agency staff, and other specified stakeholders: (a) organisational background; (b) humanitarian accountability framework; (c) humanitarian plan; (d) progress reports; and (e) complaints-handling procedures.

A humanitarian plan includes overall goals and objectives (outputs/expected results), timeframe, and linked financial summary. Progress reports include progress as measured against the humanitarian plan and financial summary – reports to be made available at agreed intervals.

2.1 The agency shall ensure that information is presented in languages, formats, and media that are accessible and comprehensible for beneficiaries and specified stakeholders.

2.2 The agency shall inform disaster-affected communities about beneficiary selection criteria and deliverables as agreed with their representatives.

2.3 The agency shall include its name and contact details in all publicly available information.

2.4 The agency shall make available information about the relevant parts of its structure, including staff roles and responsibilities.

1. What is information?

By definition, information is of value to the receiver *because* it informs. If it does not inform, it is just raw data, noise, or propaganda. Communication takes place when information flows backwards and forwards between people, and through networks. This Benchmark seeks to improve communication between an agency and its stakeholders, while focusing on the particular requirements that an agency must fulfil as a provider of information.

Disaster survivors have told HAP that the following information was of critical importance to them:

- **Information about the agency:** What are its objectives? What is its capacity to respond effectively? Who in the agency is responsible for the emergency programme?

- **Information about humanitarian plans:** How, when, and
  where will disaster survivors be consulted? Who will provide
  assistance? What will be offered? Where will it be provided?
  When will it be available? In particular, who is providing food,
  water, and health care?

Accurate, timely, and accessible data about these matters would
constitute valuable information in a humanitarian crisis.

2. Why is information important?

Sharing information and knowledge strengthens trust, increases
understanding, deepens the level of participation, and improves the
impact of an emergency response. It can also facilitate ongoing
dialogue with a range of stakeholders, which in turn can lead to
better co-ordination and effectiveness.

The provision of information by an agency to its stakeholders in an
accurate and timely way is the key to meeting the principle of
transparency. Traditionally, the emphasis has been on upwards
accountability to donors, while information dissemination to other
stakeholders, such as potential beneficiaries, has been weaker.

Some stakeholders, such as institutional donors, have the power to
ensure that they receive information on a regular basis. Donors have
tended to increase the level of planning detail that they require in
funding applications, and funding contracts usually require their
partners to submit plans and reports in accordance with an agreed
schedule and format. Donors often know more about the relief
programme than its intended beneficiaries do. Yet a failure to share
information with beneficiaries in a timely manner can have very
damaging consequences. It can contribute to:

- **Confusion and delays:** There may be chaos at distribution
  time, with no one knowing who is entitled to what.
- **Waste:** The agency may waste money on unsuitable and
  inappropriate items if it does not share information with
  beneficiaries in advance.

- **Increased insecurity and violence:** Distributions may inadvertently exacerbate inequity and escalate tensions if the process is not clear and transparent.

- **Sexual exploitation and abuse:** As cases of sexual exploitation in humanitarian operations in West Africa and elsewhere have shown, beneficiaries are vulnerable to manipulation and to the extortion of sex in exchange for aid. Knowledge of rights, including complaints and redress processes, can help to reduce opportunities for exploitation of this sort.

It is important to note that this Benchmark is about the flow of information to and from intended beneficiaries and other stakeholders in order to improve the quality of services they receive; it is not about public relations or promoting the organisation, although improved dissemination of information and the better programmes that result from improved communication can only be beneficial for an agency's image.

3. How will this Benchmark be assessed?

The means of verification for this Benchmark are set out in the Standard itself as follows.

Benchmark requirements	Means of verification
2.1 The agency shall ensure that information is presented in languages, formats, and media that are accessible and comprehensible for beneficiaries and specified stakeholders.	1 Review how the languages, formats, and media have been determined. 2 Review documentation provided on organisational background, humanitarian accountability framework, humanitarian plan and financial summary, progress reports, and complaints-handling procedures.

Benchmark requirements	Means of verification
	3 Review guidelines for information dissemination.
	4 Review information availability and accessibility.
	5 Compare languages used by intended beneficiaries, local staff, and specified stakeholders with that used in documents provided.
	6 Interview beneficiaries to verify information availability.
2.2 The agency shall inform disaster-affected communities about beneficiary selection criteria and deliverables as agreed with their representatives.	1 Demonstrate that intended beneficiaries have been informed about selection criteria and entitlements, whether through minutes of meetings, letters of agreement, information boards, or other verifiable means.
	2 Interview beneficiary representatives, beneficiaries, and agency personnel.
2.3 The agency shall include its name and contact details in all publicly available information.	1 Review contact details at appropriate and publicly accessible sites.
2.4 The agency shall make available information about the relevant parts of its structure, including staff roles and responsibilities.	1 Review availability and accessibility of information provided.

Disaggregation of beneficiaries: As with Benchmarks 3 and 5, assessment will examine how the agency ensures that the diverse needs of different groups of disaster survivors are recognised, paying particular attention to gender, age, and disability, but also to ethnicity, sexuality, and other relevant factors where prejudice and discrimination may adversely affect humanitarian outcomes. The practice of disaggregation will be reviewed through documentation (e.g. needs assessments and project appraisals), through interviews with staff, partners, and beneficiaries, and through direct observation.

Working with partners

An agency working with humanitarian partners is required to:

- demonstrate that it meets the Benchmark itself
- show that its plan for supporting partners addresses this Benchmark.

As the agency may have little direct contact with beneficiaries, arrangements may need to be made to ensure that information about the agency is passed to beneficiaries via its partners.

4. Suggestions for good practice

Developing an information strategy/plan

It is important to prepare a communications strategy before a programme is launched, so that information about the agency can be disseminated from the outset. Agencies will need to review their information plans on an ongoing basis, as the programme develops and as their own knowledge increases. An information plan could consist of the following components:

- **Guiding principles that underpin the information strategy**
  - ° Define agency standards of transparency, reliability, timeliness, etc.
  - ° Clarify which information should be covered by a non-

disclosure and restricted circulation policy. Make this policy publicly available.

° Confirm the commitment of senior management to support the strategy.

° Ensure that information is an integral part of all the activities undertaken by the agency, e.g. if an operational objective is to supply water to a camp, it will be necessary to consider the ways in which information about this will be provided to disaster-affected communities and other stakeholders.

• **Analysis of what information to share**

° Agency background, objectives, structure, and contact details

° Humanitarian accountability framework

° Humanitarian plans at each location

° Progress reports against the humanitarian plans

° Complaints-handling mechanism.

• **Analysis of who the information should be shared with (target audience)**

° Stakeholders could include intended beneficiaries, disaster-affected communities, host communities, agency staff, and other specified stakeholders.

° Assess prevailing causes and practices of discrimination in access to information (e.g. differential access to television, radio, the Internet).

° Assess the different needs of specific groups, such as women, children, elderly people, and people with disabilities or mobility restrictions.

It is essential that an agency overcomes obstacles that prevent information reaching marginalised groups within the beneficiary population. The obstacles can be structural, such as language barriers, or they may result from inequality, such as the exclusion of women and girls from decision-making fora. The agency should check whether critical information has reached all groups within the disaster-affected population and that channels for feedback are open and functional.

The agency should assess the risks that receiving information may expose people to with regard to their gender, age, and other relevant factors such as disability, ethnicity, and sexuality.

- **Analysis of when to share this information**
  - At all stages of the operation, during the design phase, start-up, implementation, evaluation, and exit
  - At regular agreed reporting times throughout the life of the project
  - When there are any significant changes to the plans.
- **Analysis of how to share this information**
  - Consider the different types of information specified in the Benchmark (organisational background, humanitarian accountability framework, humanitarian plan, progress reports, complaints-handling procedures).
  - Decide on the best method for presenting each type of information to different stakeholders. Options could include annual reports, leaflets, booklets, posters, websites, organigrams, community notice boards, billboards, photographs, workshops, role plays, meetings, verbal feedback, images, etc.
  - Adapt information to make it available in different formats (print, audiovisual, etc.) so that it will be accessible to all recipients, taking into account diversity issues such as literacy levels, gender, age, ethnicity, race, and disability.
  - Ask beneficiaries what formats they would like to receive information in.
  - When working with partners, consider what information needs to be passed to beneficiaries via the partners.
- **Risk analysis**
  - Consider the potential impact of sharing information on the security of both deliverer and receiver.

- ° In particular, consider that the risks may be different for women or men, girls or boys.
- ° Assess the consequences of non-disclosure and restricted circulation policies.
- **Editorial guidelines for information materials**
- ° Test information to ensure that it is accessible to, and understood by, the target audience.
- ° Ensure that information is relevant, useful, and accurate.
- ° Update information in a timely manner.
- ° Check that information does not mislead or cause harm to the beneficiaries or to the agency, and that it respects the dignity of all.
- ° Provide opportunities for feedback.
- **Clear and achievable (SMART) objectives and indicators**
- ° Prepare a list of information materials to be produced. This might include a summary of commissioning authority, purpose, author, format, distribution method, cost, and feedback mechanism.
- **Budget**
- ° Ensure that the costs of the information plan can be met.
- **Monitoring and evaluation process**
- ° Review and refine the information strategy at regular intervals and whenever humanitarian plans change.

5. References to further tools and information

References and links

The points made in this section are similar to the principles embodied in Common Standard 1 on participation in the Sphere Handbook, which states: 'The disaster-affected population should actively participate in the assessment, design, implementation, monitoring and evaluation of the assistance programme' (p.28). Key phrases from the indicators to this Standard refer specifically to information (e.g. people 'receive information ... and are given the opportunity to comment'). Guidance note 2 on communication and transparency states: 'The sharing of information and knowledge among all those involved is fundamental to achieving a better understanding of the problem and to providing coordinated assistance. The results of assessments should be actively communicated to all concerned organisations and individuals. Mechanisms should be established to allow people to comment on the programme e.g. by means of public meetings or via community-based organisations. For individuals who are homebound or disabled, specific outreach programmes may be required' (p.29).

The Sphere Project, *Humanitarian Charter and Minimum Standards in Disaster Response*, (2004 edition), available at: www.sphereproject.org

IASC Gender Handbook in Humanitarian Action: Women, Girls, Boys and Men – Different Needs, Equal Opportunities, available at: www.humanitarianinfo.org/iasc/content/documents

IASC, *Guidelines for Gender-based Violence Interventions in Humanitarian Settings*, available at: www.humanitarianinfo.org/iasc/content/default.asp

Building Safer Organisations: Supporting the development of NGO capacity to respond to allegations of staff misconduct, in particular in relation to abuse and exploitation of persons of concern, available at: www.hapinternational.org

Benchmark 3: Beneficiary participation and informed consent

The agency shall enable beneficiaries and their representatives to participate in programme decisions and seek their informed consent.

3.1 The agency shall specify the processes it uses to identify intended beneficiaries and their representatives with specific reference to gender, age, disability, and other identifiable vulnerabilities.

3.2 The agency shall enable intended beneficiaries and their representatives to participate in project design, implementation, monitoring, and evaluation.

1. What are participation and informed consent?

Disaster survivors are always the principal actors in a humanitarian crisis, and the involvement of aid agencies in the disaster response is a form of interference – welcome, it is hoped – in the lives of those affected. Aid agencies seek to participate in and contribute to the struggle of people affected by disaster to survive and, ideally, they should enjoy the informed consent of the people they are privileged to be in a position to help. Participation is the process through which disaster survivors can be empowered to actively exercise their right to informed consent.

The concepts of participation and empowerment are closely intertwined. Empowerment is sometimes described as the ability to make choices, but it must also include the ability to shape the choices on offer. Empowerment does not necessarily mean reversing existing realities (such as challenging power hierarchies or disempowering agencies); rather, it is about enabling people affected by disasters to make their own choices, to speak out on their own behalf, and to control their own lives. Participation and informed consent are key processes in achieving this.

The HAP Standard highlights two aspects of participation:

- **Participation in programme decisions:** Individual or community representatives actively engage in decision-making processes throughout the project cycle. However, because of the disaster context itself or due to pre-existing power differentials (e.g. based on gender, race, class, caste, etc.), participation may not occur spontaneously. Instead, it may need to be stimulated and facilitated, and aid agencies may have to foster a process of mutual learning and dialogue. Particular attention needs to be given to people traditionally excluded from power and decision-making processes, e.g. women, children, elderly people, people with disabilities, landless or homeless people, and ethnic, racial, and religious groups (not necessarily in a minority). Specific opportunities and facilitation may have to be provided to enable people accustomed to exclusion to participate in an active and meaningful manner.

- **Informed consent:** An individual or a community (through representation) gives its consent (expressed willingness, permission, or voluntary agreement) to programme activity based upon an appreciation and understanding of the facts and implications of an action.

2. Why are participation and informed consent important?

Participation entails mobilisation of the leadership and skills found within affected communities, so that disaster survivors are better able to define their priorities and determine their own fate. Participation also makes for more effective programming based on a sound understanding of the local context and culture. It increases trust and co-operation, and communities affected by disaster are seen to recover more quickly if they are active participants, and are able to regain some control over even small aspects of their lives. Effective participation at the design stage will mean more effective programmes, while participation during implementation will increase efficiency through reducing waste and losses.

Participation in monitoring and evaluation will streamline the learning cycle and encourage adaptive responses. Participation will also reduce complaints and the costs of providing compensation, because it will help to identify and thus avoid potential vulnerabilities to accidents and damage, as well as building support for the project from affected populations.

3. How will this Benchmark be assessed?

The means of verification for this Benchmark are set out in the Standard itself as follows.

Benchmark requirements	Means of verification
3.1 The agency shall specify the processes it uses to identify intended beneficiaries and their representatives with specific reference to gender, age, disability, and other identifiable vulnerabilities.	1 Review mechanism used to identify and disaggregate intended beneficiaries. 2 Review processes used to enable participation. 3 Interview staff about the processes for enabling participation.
3.2 The agency shall enable intended beneficiaries and their representatives to participate in project design, implementation, monitoring, and evaluation.	1 Demonstrate how its analysis of capacity has influenced implementation. 2 Review the appointment process of beneficiary representatives. 3 Review actual beneficiary input and impact on project design, implementation, monitoring, and evaluation. 4 Review the process used for establishing beneficiary criteria. 5 Review records of meetings held with beneficiary representatives.

Working with partners

An agency working with humanitarian partners is required to:

- show that the agency itself ensures beneficiary participation and informed consent in its dealings with beneficiaries, however limited these may be, e.g. field visits, evaluations

- show that its strategy for supporting partners addresses this Benchmark.

4. Suggestions for good practice

Participation has come to mean many different things, ranging from a minimalist approach of simply informing beneficiaries what they are to be given (where participation is reduced to the act of consumption) through to cash distributions designed to transfer to survivors the right to choose for themselves how to use the assistance offered. As a rule of thumb, this latter approach is to be commended as it reflects two important propositions. First, that people are normally the best judges of their own welfare, and second, that autonomous decision-making is an inherent element of human dignity.

Participation and informed consent are important ideals but they are not always easy to achieve, and success depends upon two factors in particular:

- Agency-wide recognition and commitment to their importance

- Participation that offers genuine engagement rather than tokenistic involvement.

Consider the following when seeking informed consent:

- **Needs assessment interviews:** Interviews with disaster-affected people are about soliciting and providing information, in accordance with Benchmark 2. It is good practice to ask for feedback after sharing information, e.g. was the information understandable, timely, and safe? Exchanges and discussions can be minuted formally or documented informally, depending on the situation. Confidentiality and safety must always be considered, and appropriate measures taken.

- **Beneficiary selection criteria:** The disaster-affected community and the agency need to work together to agree a set of criteria for beneficiary selection. Communication of these criteria is vital once they have been agreed. It is particularly important to include women in this process so that beneficiaries who might otherwise remain excluded are identified, e.g. single women, women-headed family groups/households, and child-headed households.

- **Participatory evaluation:** The project outcome should be evaluated jointly with disaster survivors in order to obtain an accurate picture and to learn lessons for the future.

- **Complaints-handling:** Inevitably, some disaster survivors will either not receive all the information necessary or will disagree with the decisions that are taken. An accessible and safe complaints-handling system will make it easier to deal with any complaints that arise (see Benchmark 5).

- **Verifying informed consent:** Verifying whether informed consent has been granted or whether levels of participation are adequate can be complex and difficult. People may express consent without fully understanding all the implications or without having a comprehensive grasp of the issues. A degree of consent and participation may have to be assumed, based on observation, knowledge, or legal or other documents (e.g. contractual agreements with the community).

- **Co-ordination:** As far as possible, the informed consent of intended beneficiaries should be sought in full knowledge of official policies and plans, as well as the plans and activities of other agencies. It is therefore desirable to identify all agencies operating or planning to operate in the area and to share this information with disaster survivors and officials. In general, the closer that co-ordination decisions are made to the disaster-affected population the better.

5. References to further tools and information

Tools

Annex 3 includes the following useful tools:

- Tool 1: How accountable are you? Checking public information
- Tool 2: How to decide whether to do a survey
- Tool 3: How to assess child protection needs
- Tool 4: How to start using indicators
- Tool 10: How to introduce your agency: a need-to-know check-list
- Tool 11: How to profile the affected community and assess initial needs
- Tool 12: How to conduct an individual interview
- Tool 14: How to involve people throughout the project
- Tool 15: How to conduct a focus group
- Tool 16: How to say goodbye
- Tool 17: Heart of community engagement
- Tool 18: Making a consultation meeting effective
- Tool 19: Participation strategy framework
- Tool 29: How to hold a lessons-learned meeting

References and links

This section draws on the following materials:

The Sphere Project (2004), *Humanitarian Charter and Minimum Standards in Disaster Response,* available at: www.sphereproject.org

> Common Standard 1 on participation: 'The disaster-affected population actively participates in the assessment, design, implementation, monitoring and evaluation of the assistance programme' (p.28).

Common Standard 2 on initial assessment: 'Assessments provide an understanding of the disaster situation and a clear analysis of threats to life, dignity, health, and livelihoods to determine, in consultation with the relevant authorities, whether an external response is required and, if so, the nature of the response' (p.29).

Common Standard 4 on targeting: 'Humanitarian assistance or services are provided equitably and impartially, based on the vulnerability and needs of individuals or groups affected by disaster' (p.35). Key phrases of relevance are also contained in the indicators, and further details are contained in the guidance notes on targeting mechanisms and targeting criteria (pp.36–7).

Common Standard 5 on monitoring: 'The effectiveness of the programme in responding to problems is identified and changes in the broader context are continually monitored, with a view to improving the programme, or to phasing it out as required' (p.37). A number of key phrases of relevance are also contained in the indicators (pp.37–8).

Common Standard 6 on evaluation: 'There is a systematic and impartial examination of humanitarian action, intended to draw lessons to improve practice and policy and to enhance accountability' (p.39). A number of key phrases of relevance are also contained in the indicators (pp.39–40).

ALNAP (2003) *Participation by Crisis Affected Populations: A Handbook for Practitioners*, Overseas Development Institute, London, available at:
www.alnap.org/publications/gs_handbook/gs_handbook.pdf
IASC Gender Handbook in Humanitarian Action: Women, Girls, Boys and Men – Different Needs, Equal Opportunities, available at:
www.humanitarianinfo.org/iasc/content/documents

IASC, *Guidelines for Gender-based Violence Interventions in Humanitarian Settings,* available at: www.humanitarianinfo.org/iasc/content/default.asp

Building Safer Organisations: Supporting the development of NGO capacity to respond to allegations of staff misconduct, in particular in relation to abuse and exploitation of persons of concern, available at: www.hapinternational.org

Benchmark 4: Competent staff

The agency shall determine the competencies, attitudes, and development needs of staff required to implement its humanitarian quality management system

4.1 The agency shall maintain a statement of the competencies (knowledge, skills, and behaviours) and attitudes required from its staff.

4.2 The agency shall ensure that staff are aware of the humanitarian accountability framework and humanitarian quality management system, their relevance and importance, and that they understand their responsibilities in their implementation.

4.3 The agency shall implement a system to review staff performance and competencies, including their knowledge, skills, behaviours, and attitudes.

4.4 The agency shall enable continual staff development for more effective implementation of the humanitarian quality management system.

1. What are competencies?

The term 'competencies' refers to all experience, skills, and behaviours that an individual may bring to their job, including – and in addition to – experience and technical skills. But it also defines how individuals are expected to fulfil their roles, and how they will be held accountable.

2. Why are staff competencies important?

No matter how good an agency's management system is or how noble its intentions, the agency is only as good as its staff. An agency's human resources are its most important asset, but also a source of potential risk. The competencies of staff will greatly affect the quality of services received by disaster-affected populations. Human resource management during humanitarian crises can be very difficult: standard recruitment procedures and checks may be relaxed because of the surge in demand and the lack of availability of qualified personnel at short notice; moreover, staff may be expected to perform duties in dangerous and chaotic circumstances, with minimum supervision.

While compassion and a respect for beneficiaries are fundamental attributes in a humanitarian worker, these need to be matched with the knowledge and skills necessary to do the job effectively and efficiently. Adequate systems need to be in place for recruiting, training, supervising, and supporting staff. Sometimes it may be necessary to respond to a new emergency with a less than optimal cadre of staff, but adequate training and support need to follow quickly to bring staff up to the required level. Furthermore, as well as the agency's responsibilities to beneficiaries, it also has a duty of care towards the people it employs.

In summary, there are three major drivers of the Benchmark on competent staff:

* Providing optimal services for disaster-affected communities and ensuring that they are protected from further danger and exploitation, e.g. cases of sexual exploitation by aid workers.
* Protection of humanitarian staff themselves.
* Protection of the image and reputation of the agency.

Although this Benchmark focuses on staff competencies and the requirements and means of verification, it also looks at the practices the agency seeks to apply within its recruitment policy, in particular with regards to equal opportunities. This would include good practice in seeking to achieve gender balance in staff composition and leadership.

3. How will this Benchmark be assessed?

The means of verification for this Benchmark are set out in the Standard itself as follows.

Benchmark requirements	Means of verification
4.1 The agency shall maintain a statement of the competencies (knowledge, skills, and behaviours) and attitudes required from its staff.	1 Review job descriptions, recruitment files, and vacancy notices. 2 Interview agency staff responsible for recruitment, assignment, and training.
4.2 The agency shall ensure that staff are aware of the humanitarian accountability framework and the humanitarian quality management system, their relevance and importance, and that they understand their responsibilities in their implementation.	1 Review induction and briefing procedures. 2 Interview staff to check awareness.
4.3 The agency shall implement a system to review staff performance and competencies, including their knowledge, skills, behaviours, and attitudes.	1 Review the performance management system. 2 Review performance appraisal documents and other formal approaches. 3 Review follow-up activities. 4 Interview staff to check the impact of appraisal and performance management.
4.4 The agency shall enable continual staff development for more effective implementation of the humanitarian quality management system.	1 Review staff training records. 2 Review other staff development approaches. 3 Review agency support for the continual improvement of its humanitarian partners.

Working with partners

An agency working with humanitarian partners is required to:

* show that the agency is itself meeting this Benchmark;
* show that its plan for supporting partners addresses this Benchmark.

4. Suggestions for good practice

Competent staff are essential throughout an operation. All staff should have a current job description before they start work, and training should be provided on an ongoing basis to ensure that staff have the requisite skills and knowledge. Regular performance reviews are also important.

Basics

At a minimum, a quality management system that prioritises humanitarian accountability will need to:

* Keep job descriptions and staff competency statements up to date.

* Implement a performance management system (i.e. ongoing verification that staff are fulfilling their roles professionally, effectively, and efficiently) that takes into account the context of the emergency and the timeframe of the project. Appraisal schedules must be flexible enough to cover projects that last only a few months as well as those that last for years.

* Implement a training plan that covers key general topics, including the humanitarian accountability framework, as well as more job-specific identified training needs.

* Monitor and evaluate the effectiveness of these procedures.

Recruitment policies should include equal opportunities, and non-discrimination guidance.

Staff competencies

There are a number of general roles commonly found within humanitarian agencies: project manager, administrator, finance officer, logistician, sectoral manager, sector specialist, and so on. There may be some variations in these roles depending on the nature and location of the emergency and the type of response being mounted, but nevertheless a common set of humanitarian competencies can be identified. Preparing a standardised set of competencies required for each role will facilitate the rapid creation of context-specific job descriptions. Stating the competencies necessary for any role will give a clear indication of the combination of skills and experience necessary. Competencies are often broken down into:

* required knowledge
* professional skills
* personal qualities.

Comparing applicants' CVs with the job description may reveal gaps that will need to be addressed through training, coaching, mentoring, or supervision.

Performance management and training

Effective performance management will help the agency to comply with Benchmark 4. Training can often be overshadowed by busy schedules, urgent deadlines, and a sense that other activities are more important for saving lives. Committing to and setting up a systematic approach to staff development and performance improvement may seem daunting, but many organisations already have excellent tools that may just need minor adjustments for use in emergency situations. The following suggestions may help in making appropriate adaptations to performance management systems:

* Use the job description set of competencies as a self-assessment checklist that staff members can complete themselves to ascertain

how confident they feel about their role and what training they require. The supervisor/line manager can then review this at the beginning of the recruitment process and plan any training needs identified.

- Training can take many forms, such as:
  - ° coaching and mentoring (one of the most effective methods)
  - ° internal training courses (a combination of classroom and practical learning)
  - ° external training courses
  - ° self-teaching, e.g. reading required material and familiarisation with guidelines and processes used by the agency.
- People's abilities can be verified by observing them, reviewing their work output, interviewing colleagues and beneficiaries, and through formal and informal appraisals.
- Findings can then be updated on the performance assessment list and any gaps dealt with before the next appraisal.
- It is the responsibility of the agency to monitor and evaluate whether these processes are occurring and to ensure that managers are trained to carry out appraisals and to manage performance.

Record-keeping

A minimum amount of recording-keeping is essential. This is not just to meet audit requirements, but also to protect beneficiaries, staff, and the agency. Record-keeping ensures continuity, improves communication, and facilitates good planning.

5. References to further tools and information

Tools

See the following Tool in Annex 3 for further assistance:

- Tool 20: Performance assessment checklists.

References and links

People in Aid, People in Aid Code of Practice, available at:
www.peopleinaid.org.uk/

HAP, *Humanitarian Accountability: Key Elements and Operational Framework*, available at:
www.HAPinternational.org/pdf_word/335-Final%20Operational %20framework.pdf

The Sphere Project (2004), Humanitarian Charter and Minimum Standards In Disaster Response (2004 edition), available at:
www.sphereproject.org

One World Trust, Global Accountability Project (GAP), available at:
www.oneworldtrust.org/?display=gapframework

Benchmark 5: Complaints-handling

The agency shall establish and implement complaints-handling procedures that are effective, accessible, and safe for intended beneficiaries, disaster-affected communities, agency staff, humanitarian partners, and other specified bodies.

5.1 The agency shall ask intended beneficiaries and the host community about appropriate ways to handle complaints.

5.2 The agency shall establish and document complaints-handling procedures which clearly state:
  - the right of beneficiaries and other specified stakeholders to file a complaint
  - the purpose, parameters, and limitations of the procedure
  - the procedure for submitting complaints
  - the steps taken in processing complaints
  - confidentiality and non-retaliation policy for complainants
  - the process for safe referral of complaints that the agency is not equipped to handle
  - the right to receive a response.

5.3 The agency shall ensure that intended beneficiaries, affected communities, and its staff understand the complaints-handling procedures.

5.4 The agency shall verify that all complaints received are handled according to the stated procedures.

5.5 The agency shall establish and implement an effective and safe complaints-handling mechanism for its staff, consistent with the requirements set out in 5.2.

1. What is complaints-handling?

Accountability involves a two-way flow, a dialogue: it is about the right to have a say and the duty to respond. This means that stakeholders should have the opportunity to ask questions and give feedback on whatever is important to them, and that the agency should then respond to these concerns.

Being accountable to beneficiaries requires that humanitarian agencies take account of beneficiaries' opinions, concerns, suggestions, and complaints. Most communication from disaster-affected people consists of advice and information, which agencies can adopt, challenge, or disregard as appropriate. A complaint, by contrast, contains the specific grievance of a stakeholder who believes that a humanitarian agency has failed to meet a stated commitment. This commitment can relate to a project plan, beneficiary criteria, an activity schedule, a standard of technical performance, an organisational value, a legal requirement, staff performance or behaviour, or any other point. While responding to feedback may be optional, a complaint requires an answer. It is the agency's responsibility to solicit both feedback and complaints, and to ensure that factors preventing disaster survivors from raising concerns are minimised and addressed.

An effective complaints-handling procedure will be accessible to, and safe for, all stakeholders. Agencies should bear in mind the vulnerability to manipulation, exploitation, and exclusion experienced by particular groups. Within any disaster-affected group, large or small, there will be power dynamics and political, social, and cultural norms that impact directly on peoples' opportunity to participate. At a minimum, agencies must seek to prevent social, political, ethnic, religious, disability, gender and age discrimination from adversely affecting the impartiality of their humanitarian work. Particular attention should always be paid to the specific needs of women and children, and to their voices in consultation processes. As effective complaints-handling is essential for improving the quality of humanitarian work, special measures to ensure that complaints procedures are accessible to the most vulnerable and socially excluded may be required. Methods for soliciting feedback and complaints should be culturally and socially appropriate (e.g. ensuring that female staff seek feedback from female beneficiaries in circumstances where it is culturally unacceptable for women to talk to an unrelated man), and that they provide a variety of means for giving feedback and submitting complaints for those who are unable to read or write or articulate their concerns for any other reason (e.g. people with hearing or speech impediments, children, different language groups)

It should also be noted that this Benchmark requires a complaints procedure that is accessible to other stakeholders, most notably agency staff and humanitarian partners. A grievance procedure should be in place to deal with staff complaints, and a system for dealing with problems and concerns between the agency and its humanitarian partners should be instituted.

2. Why are complaints mechanisms important?

The reality of humanitarian situations means that sometimes beneficiaries may be unable to complain due to fear of retaliation (real or perceived), because of a lack of knowledge, opportunity, or trust, or because of a sense of hopelessness. An accountable agency should consider complaints-handling as a positive process that can:

- provide an early indicator that a process or plan is not working
- safely highlight a concern within a community
- provide a non-judicial, respectful means for addressing grievances
- increase transparency
- demonstrate an agency's humility and commitment to achieving its goals
- improve security
- provide valuable management information
- protect the dignity of users
- highlight cases of fraud, inefficiency, or abuse.

Evidence from both the profit and non-profit sectors strongly indicates that soliciting and handling complaints effectively leads to better relations between the client (in this case the disaster-affected person) and the service provider, and also leads to better-quality and more cost-effective service provision.

3. How will this Benchmark be assessed?

The means of verification for this Benchmark are set out in the Standard itself as follows.

Benchmark requirements	Means of verification
5.1 The agency shall ask intended beneficiaries and the host community about appropriate ways to handle complaints.	1 Demonstrate that findings from consultations have been incorporated into complaints-handling procedures.
5.2 The agency shall establish and document complaints-handling procedures which clearly state: • the right of beneficiaries and other specified stakeholders to file a complaint • the purpose, parameters, and limitations of the procedure. • the procedure for submitting complaints • the steps taken in processing complaints • confidentiality and non-retaliation policy for complainants • the process for safe referral of complaints that the agency is not equipped to handle • the right to receive a response	1 Review the documented procedures. 2 Review samples of complaints to verify that complainants have been able to understand and use the procedure. 3 Review budget, contracts, and support provided to humanitarian partners to implement this requirement. 4 Interview field staff, affected community members, and/or intended beneficiaries about their perceptions and the adequacy of the procedures.

Benchmark requirements	Means of verification
5.3 The agency shall ensure that intended beneficiaries, affected communities, and its staff understand the complaints-handling procedures.	1 Review strategy and activities for raising awareness among these groups of their right to file a complaint and the procedures to use. 2 Review documents about the complaints-handling procedures made available to intended beneficiaries. 3 Interview staff, affected community members, and/or intended beneficiaries to verify awareness of and adequacy of the procedures and confidence in their integrity.
5.4 The agency shall verify that all complaints received are handled according to the stated procedures.	1 Review a sample of both pending and processed complaints, to check the integrity of the system. 2 Review reports on the integrity of the complaints-handling process.
5.5 The agency shall establish and implement an effective and safe complaints-handling mechanism for its staff, consistent with the requirements set out in 5.2.	1 Review the procedure and samples of complaints made. 2 Interview staff to verify awareness of procedure and confidence in its integrity.

Working with partners

While the agency being audited can take the approach of *promoting* compliance by humanitarian partners with regards to most of the benchmarks contained in the HAP standard, there are stricter expectations as far as Benchmark 5 is concerned.

An agency working with humanitarian partners is required to:

*   set up its own complaints-handling procedures which enable beneficiaries, partners, staff, and other stakeholders to lodge complaints;

*   ensure that its humanitarian partners are implementing agreed complaints-handling procedures which enable beneficiaries to complain to the partner but also to the agency directly. The 'good practice' section below provides suggestions on how to establish complaints-handling procedures involving partners.

4. Suggestions for good practice

Establishing a complaints-handling mechanism

Ideally, a complaints procedure should be set up at the start of all programmes and should run throughout the project. Although many programmes will have been set up without such procedures, it is still better to set them up later than not at all.

One of the main fears of many practitioners when thinking about setting up a complaints mechanism is that they will be inundated with complaints that they are unable to address, because they concern issues outside the agency's remit or responsibility. In practice, a more common problem is the under-utilisation of complaints-handling procedures.

Design of procedures

Complaints procedures can be simple, although they need to be carefully planned and need to follow certain key principles. A badly designed or managed complaints procedure can be harmful. Mechanisms to handle complaints should consider the following:

- Staff should understand, appreciate, and accept the agency's commitment to a complaints-handling policy.

- Prior to setting up a complaints-handling mechanism, a thorough analysis of the context should take place, incorporating the needs of the specific programme/sector. For example, a complaints-handling mechanism for a health programme will require a different emphasis to one for a non-food distribution programme.

- Beneficiaries should have the right to complain about anything linked to the agency's work and commitments, e.g. humanitarian accountability framework commitments, humanitarian plans, quality of delivery of the services/assistance, behaviour of staff. Where national or international law has been broken, a clear referral system should be in place.

- All allegations of staff misconduct received from beneficiaries or other staff must be investigated according to the official investigation procedures of the agency. Agencies should have formal investigation procedures that adhere to the principles of confidentiality, independence, and respect. Investigations must be conducted in a thorough, professional manner and must meet legal standards. The *Building Safer Organisations* guidelines on receiving and investigating allegations of sexual abuse and exploitation by humanitarian workers provide details of the investigation process (see references below).

- Although complaints may have common features, each one is unique and should be dealt with as such.

- Information systems and complaints mechanisms are linked; often complaints may arise because of a lack of information.

- Agencies should actively solicit complaints from beneficiaries. Soliciting complaints makes it clear that the agency is willing to provide redress, when it is justified.

- The procedures and parameters of the complaints system should be clearly understood by all potential users. Particular effort is needed to communicate these to marginalised groups.

- Beneficiaries should be told about the complaints-handling mechanism and should have the confidence to use it, knowing that their concerns will be answered. This will only be the case if there is mutual trust.

- No complaint should be ignored.

Working with humanitarian partners

Complaints-handling procedures for agencies working through humanitarian partners require special consideration. The procedure will need to allow beneficiaries to complain to the humanitarian partner and to the agency itself, and must also enable the humanitarian partner to complain to the agency about any concerns it has. The agency should develop a complaints-handling procedure to be adopted and used by humanitarian partners which:

- outlines the process by which the humanitarian partner can complain to the agency, and vice versa

- is based on consultation with partners, so that appropriate methods are used in handling complaints

- is documented, accessible, and understandable to partners, and includes:

  ○ the rights of beneficiaries to make a complaint

  ○ the purpose, parameters, and limitations of the procedure

  ○ details on how to submit a complaint

  ○ the steps to be followed once the complaint is submitted

  ○ assurances of confidentiality and non-retaliation (particularly for complaints relating to gender-based violence and sexual exploitation and abuse, given the social stigma associated with these and the very real danger that women/children reporting such abuse could face from perpetrators, or from their own families and communities)

  ○ a commitment to refer complaints that the humanitarian partner and agency are unable to handle

° a commitment by the humanitarian partner and agency to give a response

° the right of beneficiaries to complain directly to the agency instead of going through the humanitarian partner (contact details of the agency should be given on all information materials concerning the complaints-handling procedure).

5. References to further tools and information

Tools

See the following Tools in Annex 3 for further assistance:

- Tool 22: Complaints mechanisms: tips on file storage and data management
- Tool 23: Community feedback system: complaints cards
- Tool 24: How to set up a complaints and response mechanism
- Tool 25: Notes and guidelines about complaints-handling
- Tool 26: Points to remember when implementing a complaints-handling mechanism
- Tool 27: Step-by-step guide to setting up a complaints mechanism

References and links

Keeping Children Safe: www.keepingchildrensafe.org.uk

Childwise: www.childwisenet/choose-with-care.php

IASC Gender Handbook in Humanitarian Action: Women, Girls, Boys and Men – Different Needs, Equal Opportunities, available at: www.humanitarianinfo.org/iasc/content/documents

IASC, *Guidelines for Gender-based Violence Interventions in Humanitarian Settings*, available at: www.humanitarianinfo.org/iasc/content/default.asp

Building Safer Organisations: Supporting the development of NGO capacity to respond to allegations of staff misconduct, in particular in relation to abuse and exploitation of persons of concern, available at: www.hapinternational.org

Benchmark 6: Continual improvement

The agency shall establish a process of continual improvement for its humanitarian accountability framework and humanitarian quality management system.

6.1   The agency shall specify the processes used for continual improvement of:
- the agency's humanitarian accountability framework
- the agency's humanitarian quality management system, inclusive of all HAP Benchmarks.

6.2   The agency shall together with its humanitarian partners monitor and evaluate the agreed means to improve the quality of the partnership with respect to the Principles of Accountability and the Principles for Humanitarian Action.

1. What is continual improvement?

Learning from past successes and failures and applying these insights to modify and adapt future work is a cornerstone of accountability. A culture of learning and continual improvement should lie at the heart of a professional and committed agency. Continual improvement is achieved through an effective monitoring and evaluation system, which ensures regular reviews of the work of the agency, its impact, and effectiveness, and which identifies lessons for improving future operations.

2. Why is continual improvement important?

No product or service is ever perfect, either because it is produced less efficiently than it could be, or because it could be better adapted to meet the needs of the customer. This reality holds equally good for disaster survivors and humanitarian agencies. Therefore, the search for continual improvement must be an integral part of the humanitarian enterprise if it is to achieve optimum levels of service to disaster survivors. Its realisation will also benefit its staff members as donors will be assured that their funds are being used effectively, and the agency itself and the humanitarian sector as a whole will consequently enjoy a strengthened reputation based on the confidence and trust of its stakeholders.

3. How will this Benchmark be assessed?

The Standard requires that the agency identifies its starting point and then shows how it plans to improve the quality of its humanitarian services. The Benchmarks are starting points only: agencies are expected to build and develop from them. The degree to which agencies have improved will be a particular focus in subsequent audits for surveillance or re-certification. The way in which this Benchmark is tied in with Benchmark 1 is explained in the section on Benchmark 1 above.

The means of verification for this Benchmark are set out in the Standard itself as follows.

Benchmark requirements	Means of verification
6.1 The agency shall specify the processes used for continual improvement of: • the agency's humanitarian accountability framework • the agency's humanitarian quality management system, inclusive of all HAP Benchmarks.	1 Review continual improvement process document/system. 2 Note the dates when it was created and last updated. 3 Dissemination: note if the latest version is accessible at all levels within the agency. 4 Review meeting agendas and minutes to note discussions held and decisions taken to improve processes. 5 Demonstrate how lessons learned impact current processes. 6 Review feedback from governing bodies. 7 Review internal and external audits and evaluations pertinent to the agency and how evaluation recommendations are acted upon and learning is incorporated.

Benchmark requirements	Means of verification
6.2 The agency shall together with its humanitarian partners monitor and evaluate the agreed means to improve the quality of the partnership with respect to the Principles of Accountability and the Principles for Humanitarian Action.	**1** Review improvement plans (agreed actions, strategies for learning) for partners, noting date of drafting. **2** Review monitoring and evaluation reports and note impact on improvement plan. **3** Review partner contracts and note inclusion of relevant contractual support and expectations of both parties.

Working with partners

An agency working with humanitarian partners is required to:

- demonstrate that it meets the requirements itself;
- show that its plan for supporting partners addresses this Benchmark;
- show how it monitors the progress of its partners.

4. Suggestions for good practice

Process design

Continual improvement is an essential part of quality assurance and should thus be a part of all activities, both strategic and in day-to-day management. Continual improvement should start at the very beginning of the project cycle, continue through implementation, and be a feature at its end.

- Continual improvement should be built into the design of the project. Project developers should take into account the organisation's humanitarian accountability framework when writing their proposals and should plan goals, objectives, and indicators accordingly.

- Regular internal and external monitoring and evaluation should take place during implementation to track lessons learned, correct mistakes, and address weaknesses.
- A final project evaluation should take place once the project is over. In addition, a review of the agency's humanitarian accountability framework and quality management system should occur, and any necessary revisions should be made.

Criteria for success

Ensuring continual improvement in the quality of humanitarian services requires that:

- Beneficiaries and other stakeholders are included in the monitoring and evaluation process.
- Senior management demonstrate a commitment to continual improvement in the agency's strategic objectives and in its allocation of resources.
- The improvement process is adapted to each level of management. For example, a large international NGO might apply the following approach:
  - Head office level: review strategy and quality management system (e.g. review cycle could be every three to five years, with annual monitoring)
  - Regional level: review strategy and quality management system (e.g. annually, with monitoring every three to four years)
  - Country level: review quarterly, with monthly monitoring
  - Project level: review monthly, with weekly monitoring
  - In emergencies, a shorter review cycle is applied (e.g. weekly with daily monitoring)
  - Internal and external monitoring and evaluation of specific programmes/projects should be supplementary to the review processes described above.

- Quality assurance of the system means that managers throughout the system are responsible for ensuring that each level is complying and reporting.

- Problems (current or potential) need to be captured, then discussed in designated management meetings at each level. Follow-up and follow-through actions should be agreed, implemented, monitored, and reviewed.

- Lessons learned should become part of the knowledge management system, and should be shared throughout the agency.

- Responsible innovation is encouraged throughout the humanitarian project cycle.

5. References to further tools and information

Tools

See the following Tools in Annex 3 for further assistance:

- Tool 4: How to start using indicators
- Tool 5: How to give a verbal report
- Tool 6: Plan–do– check–act quality assurance cycle (PDCA)
- Tool 7: SWOT analysis (strengths, weaknesses, opportunities, and threats)
- Tool 10: How to introduce your agency: a need-to-know checklist
- Tool 13: How to observe
- Tool 15: How to conduct a focus group
- Tool 16: How to say goodbye
- Tool 24: How to set up a complaints and response mechanism
- Tool 28: Corrective and preventative action plan tracking guide
- Tool 29: How to hold a lessons learned meeting

References and links

This section draws on:

The Sphere Project (2004), *Humanitarian Charter and Minimum Standards in Disaster Response,* Common Standard 6 on evaluation: 'There is a systematic and impartial examination of humanitarian action, intended to draw lessons to improve practice and policy and to enhance accountability' (p.39).

The Sphere Project (2004), *Humanitarian Charter and Minimum Standards In Disaster Response* available at: www.sphereproject.org

One World Trust, Global Accountability Project (GAP), available at: www.oneworldtrust.org/?display=gapframework

Notes

1 J. Pictet (1979) 'The Fundamental Principles of the Red Cross – Commentary', ICRC: Geneva.

2 SMART means specific, measurable, achievable, relevant/realistic, and time-bound.

3 The *Code of Conduct for the International Red Cross Movement and NGOs in Disaster Relief* (1994) was also an important source, especially with regard to Principle 7: 'Ways shall be found to involve programme beneficiaries in the management of relief aid'; Principle 9: 'We hold ourselves accountable to both those we seek to assist and those from whom we accept resources'; and Principle 10: 'In our information, publicity and advertising activities, we shall recognise disaster victims as dignified humans, not hopeless objects'. However, the full text of the Code of Conduct does not lend itself to use in a compliance verification audit, and as the Principles are not ranked in importance, the Code is of limited utility in exonerating non-compliance.

4 J. Pictet (1979) 'The Fundamental Principles of the Red Cross – Commentary', ICRC: Geneva.

5 Further discussion on 'The rationale for introducing a hierarchy of principles – particularly its operational impact' is available on the HAP website: www.hapinternational.org.

6 P. F. Drucker (1986) I*nnovation and Entrepreneurship: Practice and Principles,* New York: Harper Row.

Part III: The HAP Certification Scheme

5. What is the scheme and how does it work?

Overview of the HAP Certification Scheme

Expression of interest

An agency will register its preliminary interest in HAP Certification through submitting a short statement of intent to undertake a baseline analysis and a declaration of compliance with the qualifying norms for HAP Certification.

Baseline analysis

An agency with a registered interest will complete a baseline analysis of its current state of conformity with the HAP Standard.

Application

An agency requesting certification will register its interest through submission of an application file.

Document review

The audit team will review all the relevant documentation listed in the application file and submitted by the agency. Documents will need to be received by HAP at least **ten days before** the on-site audits take place.

Head office audit

A head office audit will be carried out to verify that procedures/processes specified in the documentation are being carried out. This normally takes **three days.**

Project site audit

One or more project sites (selected by the audit team) will be audited to verify that procedures/processes are being carried out at project level. These will include interviews with people affected by the disaster, staff, partners, and other specified stakeholders, where applicable.

Audit report

Based on the findings of the document review, the head office, and the project site(s) audits, the audit team will submit a report to the Certification and Accreditation Board. Observed cases of major non-compliance will delay certification until corrected. A minor non-compliance may not delay certification, but will result in a corrective action request to be undertaken by the agency within an agreed timeframe.

Introduction

Agencies may approach HAP at different stages. Some may feel that they already meet the requirements of the HAP Standard and therefore choose to apply for Certification straight away. Others may consider that they need to improve or get help in assessing their systems before they can decide whether to seek HAP Certification. This part of the Guide explains how the Certification process works, for both categories of applicants. It explains what Certification is; who carries it out; how it is carried out, and what it might cost. The box below gives a quick impression of how the scheme works.

What is Certification?

Certification is the formal evaluation of an agency against the HAP Humanitarian Accountability and Quality Management Standard (2007), using an established method to measure compliance. The strengths of the HAP Certification process are:

- independent validation of good practice with respect to humanitarian accountability and quality management;
- verification through soliciting opinions of key stakeholders, including and most importantly, people affected by disaster;
- strengthening of accountability and professionalism within the humanitarian sector;
- improvement of knowledge management and good practice throughout the agency;
- provision of an informed choice to stakeholders;

- voluntary code that enables agencies to hold themselves to account;
- appeals and complaints-handling process.

Who carries out Certification?

The HAP General Assembly is the governing body of HAP, and thus holds final authority over the content of the HAP Standard and the process of Certification. The General Assembly has delegated the responsibility for awarding HAP Certification to its Certification and Accreditation Review Board. The HAP Secretariat is charged by the General Assembly with responsibility for the continuous improvement of the Standard through ongoing consultation, research, and evaluation. It is also responsible for providing training and support in helping HAP's member agencies and new applicants to prepare for Certification.

Certification and Accreditation Review Board

The Certification and Accreditation Review Board is appointed by the HAP General Assembly and is composed of an equal number of full member representatives and independent members (i.e. having no professional affiliation with any of HAP's full members).

The HAP Secretariat provides administrative and executive support to the Certification and Accreditation Review Board. The Certification and Accreditation Review Board is responsible for:

- examining audit reports, determining whether audit recommendations are valid, and deciding whether applicants can be certified as being compliant with the HAP Standard;
- examining applications for accreditation by other bodies wishing to carry out HAP audits and determining whether this accreditation should be given;
- Holding the register of certified and accredited agencies and monitoring usage of the Certification mark/certificate.

Complaints concerning the processes of certification and accreditation, or appeals against the recommendations of the independent auditors, will be handled in the first instance by the Certification and Accreditation Review Board. If a complaint cannot be resolved to the satisfaction of all parties at this level, it will be referred to the HAP Standing Complaints Committee to be dealt with in accordance with the HAP Complaints Against Members procedure.

HAP Secretariat

The HAP Secretariat is responsible for the day-to-day management of the Certification process. This involves:

- handling all applications for Certification and accreditation:
  - managing and reviewing the application file
  - agreeing dates and locations for the audit
  - documentation
  - mid-term audit management
  - preparation of recommendations for Certification and accreditation.
- managing relations with the auditors and ensuring:
  - identification and recruitment of suitably qualified auditors
  - training of auditors to recognised HAP Standard auditing proficiency
  - accrediting and registering auditors who are proficient and qualified to audit agencies with the HAP Standard
  - allocating tasks to auditors and ensuring ongoing training and briefing for them.

HAP-registered independent auditors

Auditors used by HAP are contracted as independent consultants/auditors. They have a minimum of 5–10 years' experience in the humanitarian sector and are trained and registered as competent to audit against the HAP Standard. Only those who are accredited by HAP will be authorised to conduct HAP audits.

How is Certification carried out?

The timing of an application for Certification should be considered carefully, as the agency will first need to review the status of its quality and accountability commitments, and perhaps take a number of steps before being in a position to submit a strong application. A preliminary baseline analysis can help the agency to take stock of how well it measures up against the Standard. This should help to identify the agency's strengths and weaknesses and any changes that are needed to meet the Certification requirements. HAP provides consultancy advice at this preparatory stage, and regularly updated support material is available free of charge on the HAP website. If agencies decide not to apply for Certification, the process of self-assessment will still have been a valuable experience in identifying ways of improving the agency's quality and accountability standards. This section examines each stage of the Certification process in greater detail.

1. Expression of interest

Agencies interested in seeking HAP Certification can contact HAP to register their intent and seek further information about the requirements of the Standard and the Certification process. If the expression of interest is submitted by a non-member of HAP, this must be accompanied by a declaration of compliance with the qualifying norms for the HAP Standard, as described in Part II of this Guide. On application, HAP will provide further information and tools to help agencies decide whether they are ready to apply for Certification and what the next steps are.

Any decision to apply for Certification must be carefully considered and must enjoy the full authority of the agency. As the HAP Standard sets a number of exacting requirements, agencies are encouraged to seek advice from HAP before submitting an application. HAP can assist in conducting a baseline analysis, provide consultancy support on making improvements, and give advice on what steps should be taken in preparation for Certification.

The baseline analysis is like a 'trial audit': it will assess the current status of an agency in relation to the requirements contained in the HAP Standard. The rationale behind this is to establish whether there are any major or minor gaps in meeting the HAP Standard, estimate what time it would take to meet these, and plan accordingly. This will help to develop a realistic timeframe for meeting the HAP Standard and for conducting a successful audit.

2. Application for audit or baseline

An agency considering itself ready for Certification can submit an **application file** to the HAP Secretariat. The application file is designed to help the applicant organisation prepare for the Certification audit and ensure that all the documents needed for review by the auditors are in place. The documentation submitted will be verified by the auditors through head office and project site visits, during which they will conduct interviews and focus group discussions.

The application process and the submission requirements are very similar whether an agency is applying for a baseline analysis or for a Certification audit. The documents listed below are mandatory for agencies applying for a Certification audit; agencies applying for a baseline analysis should assemble as many of the required documents as possible, and can request further guidance from HAP in doing this.

The pro-forma **application file** can be downloaded from the HAP website. A completed application file will include the following documentation:

- **An application statement** that the agency meets the HAP Standard qualifying norms (described in Chapter 2 of this Guide), and signed by a duly authorised representative of the agency. This statement should confirm the agency's standing with regard to its:
  - ° commitment to the principle of impartiality

- ° not-for-profit status
- ° financial propriety
- ° humanitarian accountability framework.
- **Supporting documentation** to be submitted with the application statement:

1. Evidence of the agency's not-for-profit status e.g. registration as a charity or NGO, or if no independent evidence can be provided, a statement by the governing body of the agency (this is not required for HAP full members).

2. Statement of financial accountability requirements in the agency's country of incorporation or registration (not required for HAP full members).

3. Independently audited accounts for the three financial years immediately prior to the date of the application (not required for HAP full members).

4. Budget or expenditure plan for the current financial year.

5. Presentation note with summary volume and financial indicators of the level of humanitarian activity over the past three years, and a list of current humanitarian projects outlining locations, start and end dates, budget totals, and humanitarian partners.

6. Humanitarian accountability framework (if the agency is applying for a baseline analysis rather than a full audit, it can submit a draft framework that includes a list of commitments, a plan for implementation, and the agency's self-assessed baseline analysis).

7. Organisational chart (or organigram) showing governance and relevant management structures.

8. Declaration of additional interests – affiliations, interests, values etc. (See Chapter 3 on the Humanitarian Accountability Covenant for guidance).

9. Baseline analysis of compliance with the HAP Standard and improvement plan (if an agency is applying for a baseline analysis rather than an audit, it can instead confirm its intention of future compliance with the HAP Standard).

The application statement should be in English. All other documents can be in the language normally used by the agency (with a copy in English if available). Documents should be submitted by e-mail in electronic format (preferably PDF) where possible.

3. Review of application

HAP will first examine the application file for completeness. If the file is complete and the application appears satisfactory, HAP will advise the agency to request either a Certification audit or a baseline analysis. If the application is not complete, HAP may ask for additional information from the agency or suggest further steps to be taken to improve the application.

4. Audit design

On the basis of the application file, HAP will propose an audit plan and quote. The size, structure, complexity, and partnering arrangements of an agency will affect the length of the audit and project site verification requirements. The audit design will cover:

- **Location:** The audit will take place at the agency's humanitarian management and administrative centre (usually its head office) and at selected project sites.

  - **For a Certification audit:** HAP will make the final decision concerning the number and choice of project sites that will be included in the audit, although it will take account of advice offered by the agency in relation to timing of visits, travel and accommodation costs, security, and other factors affecting accessibility.

  - **For a baseline analysis:** The agency can propose which project sites will be included, although HAP reserves the right to suggest alternative locations subject to concerns relating to cost, accessibility, security, travel times, and the schedules of HAP staff and auditors.

- **Participants:** The audit will at a minimum include interviews with people affected by the disaster, senior staff, project staff, and partners where applicable.

- **Project sites not selected for audit:** These will be required to complete a short self-assessment questionnaire to be returned to HAP. This questionnaire is designed to obtain a general analysis of all operations while keeping audit costs to a minimum.

Further information concerning the rationale of audit design and its probable costs can be obtained from HAP's website (www.hapinternational.org) or by contacting the Secretariat.

5. Audit

Auditors of the HAP Standard follow audit guidelines developed by HAP. The guidelines cover the agency's head office, with a focus on policy and processes, and project sites, with a focus on verifying application. Either a single auditor or a team of two will audit head office. Auditors will be fluent in the language used by the applicant organisation in its application file. One or two auditors will audit project sites in the language customarily used by the agency at that site. If there is no auditor fluent in the relevant language available, an independent interpreter may be recruited to assist. If the management and project sites are all in one country or region, the same audit team may visit both.

6. Certification audit report

Based on the findings of the document review and the audits of head office and the project sites, the audit team will prepare a report covering the following topics:

- **Agency description**

- **Audit process**
- **Minor non-conformities:** A minor non-conformity could be due to a number of reasons, such as:
  - ° occasional failure to implement commitments
  - ° incomplete documentation and records
  - ° occasional monitoring lapses.

Minor non-conformities will not usually result in a delay of recommendation for Certification, but will require corrective action within a specified timeframe.

- **Major non-conformities:** A major non-conformity could be due to a number of reasons, such as:
  - ° serious violation of the qualifying norms
  - ° complete absence of a procedure required by the Standard
  - ° demonstrated lack of control on key quality and accountability commitments
  - ° serious defects in the quality of services, resulting in danger to beneficiaries
  - ° a series of minor non-conformities all relating to the same element of the Standard
  - ° a minor non-conformity detected in a previous audit but not addressed within the specified timeframe
  - ° false declarations of compliance.

Major non-conformities will result in a recommendation that Certification is deferred until corrective action has been taken and required improvements verified.

- **Exonerations:** When matters beyond the control or reasonable influence of the agency result in a failure to meet a requirement of the HAP Standard, exoneration can be recommended. The rationale for exoneration will refer to the Principles for Humanitarian Action set out in the HAP Standard, but may also introduce other evidence and arguments.

- **Recommendations:** A recommendation is a non-binding improvement proposition given by the auditor on matters that, if not addressed, may, in the auditor's opinion, weaken the reliability of the agency's humanitarian accountability and quality management system.

- **Observations:** The auditor may wish to draw the agency's attention to an issue noted during the audit that could impact the agency either negatively or positively. It may capture good practices, matters where improvement might be considered, or where further research or investigation is indicated, e.g. with regard to compliance with commitments that fall outside HAP's competence to assess.

- **Corrective actions:** Where non-compliance has been identified, specific time-bound corrective actions will be proposed.

- **Conclusions:** Based upon all available relevant information, the audit team will recommend to the Certification and Accreditation Review Board whether or not the agency should be awarded HAP Certification. The recommendation may be made subject to the agency agreeing to undertake the proposed corrective actions within an agreed timeframe.

The audit team will submit its report to the HAP Certification and Accreditation Manager, who will then pass it on to the Certification and Accreditation Board for a decision on Certification. Where non-compliance has been identified, time may be given for the agency to correct the inconsistency. This will be verified through a follow-up audit at the end of the period given for corrective action, and will be limited in scope to the non-conformities identified. Audit reports will remain confidential to HAP and the Certification and Accreditation Board.

7. Baseline analysis

Agencies applying for a baseline analysis rather than a Certification audit will undergo a similar process. The baseline will be carried out by HAP staff and accredited independent auditors. The process will be more collaborative and consultative than that used in a Certification audit, given that the main purpose of the analysis is to assist in improving the systems and processes of the organisation.

8. Certification

An agency recommended for Certification will receive a certificate of recognition showing that it is in compliance with the HAP Standard. The Certification and Accreditation Review Board will present the certificate and HAP Standard mark to the agency. A register of all certified agencies will be maintained and made public on the HAP website. Certification lasts for three years from the date specified on the certificate. A mandatory mid-term surveillance audit will be undertaken to validate progress. After the three-year period has expired, the agency will need to apply for re-certification to ensure continuity.

Agencies granted Certification are entitled to use the HAP Standard mark and certificate in the following ways:

- Certified agencies may use the terms 'certified' or 'certification', as well as 'registered'. They may not use the term 'accredited'.
- The mark should include reference to the HAP Standard year and title.
- Certified agencies are required to display the HAP certification mark in a prominent place on their official website and on relevant official documents.
- Certified agencies may not adapt or modify the HAP Standard mark.
- Usage of the mark should conform to the agreed guidelines.
- The mark or certificate should not be used as product guarantees.
- Reference to the scope covered by the Certification (e.g. limitations to a particular country or operation) is essential in all communications concerning the certificate. This includes usage in all geographical locations covered by the certificate.

- The mark and certificate should be removed once the Certification period is completed or replaced if the agency has undergone re-certification.

What does Certification cost?

Assessing the full 'costs' of Certification is difficult because while some costs are direct and easy to calculate (e.g. the cost of the audit), others are indirect and may involve significant 'negative costs' (i.e. benefits) that are hard to measure. This may be due to the fact that benefits can only be predicted, as they are not fully realised at the time of Certification, or it may be because the benefits are hard to measure (e.g. the valuation placed upon lives saved or dignity restored). However, no thorough appraisal of the costs of Certification would exclude such considerations, and arguably the opportunity costs of non-certification should also be assessed. These would include real although unverifiable reductions in fraud, negligence, and mismanagement, and losses due to the effect that these have on an agency's reputation, and its ability to attract donors and competent staff.

In all cases that HAP is aware of, staff and stakeholders have quickly become convinced of the overall cost/benefit case in favour of compliance with the HAP Standard, especially with regard to its impact on the quality of their humanitarian work, their relationship with their humanitarian partners and, above all, with those people the agency is assisting. HAP recommends that interested agencies should consult organisations that have achieved Certification or have engaged in significant compliance trials.

With regard to the more immediate question concerning the direct costs of Certification, the honest answer is 'it depends'. The cost of the auditing process itself is directly linked to the number of audit days and travel required to carry out both the head office and the project site visits. As an approximate guide, the charge made for the auditing process is linked to the agency's average annual expenditure. The current table of costs is available on the HAP website, and covers the following services: organisation and preparation; review of application file; audit preparation; Certification audit at head office; Certification audit at project site(s); self-assessment reviews; certificate and registration; and mandatory mid-term monitoring audit (18 months post-Certification). Flights and accommodation costs are not included and will be additional. A final quotation will be given when an application is made.

More complicated, of course, is predicting the costs of bringing an agency's systems and processes up to the level where it is able to meet the HAP Standard. A majority of agencies seeking Certification against the HAP Standard will already have a quality management system designed to improve the effectiveness and efficiency of their operations. The HAP Standard has been designed to draw attention to what are considered to be the 'mission-critical' practices that underpin accountability.

Meeting these requirements will have resource implications, particularly in terms of deploying staff dedicated to working on quality issues. The involvement of staff is essential in turning these standards into a reality, otherwise the whole process risks remaining a paper exercise. While some of the requirements of the Standard may seem burdensome, especially in the midst of a crisis, these costs must be offset against the benefits of maintaining quality standards to beneficiaries, staff, the agency, and donors. Some specific benefits of implementing the HAP Standard are:

- evidence-based rationale for beneficiary accountability and quality management
- evidence-based rationale for the selection of partners
- evidence-based rationale for identifying staff competencies and staff development needs
- evidence-based rationale for reinforcing good practices
- improved efficiency resulting from applying the principle of 'getting it right first time'.

Table 5 below presents an example of estimated resources needed to meet the HAP Standard.

Table 5: Worked example of estimated resources needed to meet the HAP Standard

Section of Standard	Staff	Timeframe
Humanitarian accountability framework (Qualifying norm 4)	1 person: senior manager Has strategy and policy oversight, and is HAP accountability focal person.	1–2 weeks to complete draft in a consultative manner.
Quality management system (Benchmark 1)	1 person: senior manager Has M&E oversight. Has management oversight.	If an agency does not have a recognised or defined humanitarian quality management system, an analysis of the agency will be required. As this is an ongoing activity, it needs to be built into a person's job description and could be linked to the internal audit/monitoring and evaluation function.
Information (Benchmark 2)	Should be a part of the responsibility of all country managers. No extra staff, just training: this could be done both through virtual training or self-teaching methods and through head office field trips/specific annual meetings, etc.	Draft policy process: 4 days. Roll-out: 12–18 months to ensure that all sites are informed/trained.

Budget	Comments
For consultants: count daily rate for 7 days. For staff: count exclusive time for 7 days.	The most time-consuming activity is not the drafting of the humanitarian accountability framework, but the baseline analysis of where the agency is currently.
If already assigned to existing staff, costs will be minimal. If it involves assigning new tasks and responsibilities, the time for this will need to be counted and budgeted.	Most agencies already have an extensive monitoring and evaluation policy and reporting structure. The quality management system may already be in place, even if it is not referred to in those terms. Benchmark 1 requires that the quality management system is documented and that the agency is able to demonstrate how it enables the humanitarian accountability framework to be implemented. This means that the initial audit will simply check that the system has been established. The surveillance audits and re-certification audits will follow up progress in more detail.
Translation and printing costs could fall under direct project costs. Costs could be a part of normal existing field trips/meetings.	Once the key information needs are decided (as per Benchmark 2, plus whatever else the agency considers important), then a standardised template can be created which can be ready for translation as needed/per context.

Section of Standard	Staff	Timeframe
Participation (Benchmark 3)	Should be a part of all field staff job descriptions. Include in briefing.	Once policy is in place, ongoing M&E and training are needed to establish habits of good practice.
Staff competencies (Benchmark 4)	HR department Field managers who deal with HR issues.	Creation of job descriptions: 1–2 days. Creation of a performance management system: 5–10 days. M&E to assess performance is a role for HR staff, along with managers.
Complaints-handling (Benchmark 5)	Line managers Sector co-ordinators Complaints-handling focal person	Set-up per site: 1 day to 1 month (depending on experience and context)
Continual improvement (Benchmark 6)	Line managers M&E team	Continual improvement may require more management follow-up.

© HAP International

Budget	Comments
Training (see Benchmark 4) Design key points to change behaviour in a methodical way.	It can be difficult to monitor and assess consistency of current practices.
Time taken to create the system. Budget for training staff: this should be developed per agency/project/strategy and incorporated into direct/indirect costs.	Training on the Standard should be included (especially) in induction courses, refresher courses, plus field trips and monitoring of appraisals. Continued staff development and training strategy will be needed.
HAP advises that 1 per cent of the budget per site should be set aside for running the complaints-handling mechanism. This budget will go mainly on a salaried position.	Drafting a policy and set of procedures/formats will take time, though some good examples exist on the HAP website. Training is key in terms of M&E.

HAP offers a variety of services to support interested agencies:

- **consultancy support:** one-to-one support for individual agencies
- **workshops:** when a particular need is identified
- **training of trainers:** developing agency resources and skills through a HAP Training of Trainers course
- **baseline assessment:** helping agencies to identify gaps and providing further support to help meet them.

Where to apply for Certification

Accreditation and Certification Manager
HAP International
Chemin Balexert 7–9
CH-1219 Châtelaine,
Geneva, Switzerland.
Tel: +41 (0)22 788 16 41
Fax: +41 (0)22 797 38 61

See website for contact details: www.hapinternational.org

General e-mail: secretariat@hapinternational.org

Annex 1: Full text of the HAP Standard

HAP Humanitarian Accountability and Quality Management Standard (2007)

Adopted by HAP on 30 January 2007

Prepared by:
HAP Editorial Steering Committee
In consultation with:
HAP Standard Development Reference Group
Beneficiary Representatives
Copenhagen Complaints Mechanism Workshop Participants
Dhaka and Nairobi Workshop Participants
Field Test Participants (Senegal, Somalia, and Sri Lanka)
© HAP International
Chemin Balexert 7–9
CH-1219 Châtelaine,
Geneva,
Switzerland.
Tel: +41 (0)22 788 16 41 Fax: +41 (0)22 797 38 61
See website for contact details: www.hapinternational.org
General e-mail: secretariat@hapinternational.org

Contents

Foreword

After more than six years of dedicated research and extensive consultation, involving so many disaster survivors, aid workers, supporters, and specialists that it is impossible to acknowledge them all individually, here at last is the HAP Humanitarian Accountability and Quality Management Standard (2007).

Above all else, I want to take this opportunity to express my heartfelt thanks to all those people who have contributed their time, energy, and knowledge to this important project, and to congratulate them on their wonderful achievement.

The essential advice distilled from the vast reservoir of wisdom and experience that fed this process can be summed up in these words; keep it simple, affordable, and effective. Above all, remember that quality management is not a new religion. It is just a practical means through which continual improvements can be made in the accountability and effectiveness of humanitarian work.

Now, all humanitarian organisations can demonstrate their commitment to this vital goal through achieving compliance with the HAP Standard and by promoting its adoption by their humanitarian partners and other actors. As a consequence, the well-being and dignity of disaster survivors will be enhanced. Surely, nothing more important could be said in commending this Standard to the humanitarian community.

With the finalisation of the HAP Standard, we can now launch the HAP Certification scheme, providing the opportunity for all committed agencies to achieve due recognition for their humanitarian quality management systems, irrespective of agency size and place of origin, and whether they implement directly or work with partners.

I invite all to participate in this exciting development.

Denis Caillaux
Chair, HAP International
Secretary-General Care International
Geneva
5 January 2007

1. Introduction

1.1 From Principles to a Standard

Humanitarian agencies exercise significant financial, technical, and logistical power in their mission to save lives and reduce suffering. In contrast, disaster survivors have no formal control and often little influence over emergency relief agencies, making it difficult for the people affected by disasters to hold these aid agencies to account. In 2003 the Humanitarian Accountability Partnership (HAP) was launched to promote accountability to disaster survivors and to acknowledge those agencies that comply with the HAP Principles of Accountability. By applying these Principles, an agency makes itself accountable to disaster survivors for the quality of its humanitarian work.

The HAP Principles of Accountability

1. Commitment to humanitarian standards and rights
- Members state their commitment to respect and foster humanitarian standards and the rights of beneficiaries.

2. Setting standards and building capacity
- Members set a framework of accountability to their stakeholders*
- Members set and periodically review their standards and performance indicators, and revise them if necessary
- Members provide appropriate training in the use and implementation of standards.

3. Communication
- Members inform, and consult with, stakeholders, particularly beneficiaries and staff, about the standards adopted, programmes to be undertaken, and mechanisms available for addressing concerns.

4. Participation in programmes
- Members involve beneficiaries in the planning, implementation, monitoring and evaluation of programmes and report to them on progress, subject only to serious operational constraints.

5. Monitoring and reporting on compliance
- Members involve beneficiaries and staff when they monitor and revise standards
- Members regularly monitor and evaluate compliance with standards, using robust processes
- Members report at least annually to stakeholders, including beneficiaries, on compliance with standards. Reporting may take a variety of forms.

6. Addressing complaints
- Members enable beneficiaries and staff to report complaints and seek redress safely.

7. Implementing partners
- Members are committed to the implementation of these principles if and when working through implementing partners.

---

* Framework of accountability includes standards, quality standards, principles, policies, guidelines, training, and other capacity-building work, etc. The framework must include measurable performance indicators. Standards may be internal to the organisation or they may be collective, e.g. Sphere or People In Aid

However, the Principles of Accountability did not include perform-ance benchmarks or verifiable compliance indicators. Nor were the 'humanitarian standards' and 'rights of beneficiaries' referred to in Principle 1 made explicit. As a consequence, the Principles of Accountability did not provide a sufficient basis to enable a consistent and coherent approach to compliance monitoring and validation of an agency's humanitarian quality management system. It has therefore been necessary to develop the HAP Humanitarian Accountability and Quality Management Standard (2007).

Like HAP's Principles of Accountability, the HAP Humanitarian Accountability and Quality Management Standard (2007) has been developed through extensive consultation and field tests. It is based upon a simple but effective humanitarian quality management system that may be applied by all humanitarian agencies. It is rooted in a set of humanitarian principles that drive and shape the humanitarian work of its adherents and by which they voluntarily elect to be held to account. As the HAP Standard represents a solemn contract to be accountable to people affected by disasters not just now but also in the future, these values are presented in the HAP Humanitarian Accountability Covenant.*

1.2 Putting Principles into Practice

The contexts in which humanitarian action takes place are complex, difficult, and sometimes hostile. More often than not, the human and financial resources at the disposal of the humanitarian community are inadequate for the task. In practice, humanitarian organisations frequently face hard choices between bad and worse options. Their aspirations to uphold the highest standards of humanitarian action cannot always be realised due to constraints beyond their control. However, the essence of humanitarianism is about acting upon the moral obligation to express solidarity with

---

* 'Covenant' is used here to denote a binding commitment.

those living in distress and suffering, even in situations when an ideal response is impossible. For example, a compassionate embrace of an earthquake victim by a neighbour has the same moral validity in humanitarian terms as a major international relief effort run by 'humanitarian professionals'. On many occasions the best possible humanitarian action may be incomplete but still worthwhile.

However, when a HAP-certified agency is unable to achieve full compliance with the Principles of Accountability, an explanation is required. The Humanitarian Accountability Covenant is a practical tool designed to provide guidance for humanitarian agencies facing tough choices. It draws upon, but is not identical to Jean Pictet's classic formulation of humanitarian principles. Each principle is categorised by its relative importance, beginning with the *primary principles* of humanity and impartiality; followed by the *secondary principles* of informed consent, duty of care, and witness; and concluding with the *tertiary principles* of independence, transparency, neutrality, and complementarity.

In certain circumstances, an agency may find that the immediate consequence of complying with one principle may render it incapable of fulfilling another. For example, the publication of a relief distribution plan may place intended beneficiaries and staff in great danger, justifying in that particular case the application of a non-disclosure policy. In cases of this kind, a HAP-certified agency must be able to explain that it chooses to operate in breach of one or more of the principles as an unavoidable condition of being able to comply with a higher-level principle in those circumstances. By so doing, the agency will have demonstrated that it acted in good faith and thus in accordance with the HAP Standard in that particular situation.

The Humanitarian Accountability Covenant also requires HAP-certified agencies to declare any additional interests or policies that may have a significant bearing upon the welfare and safety of disaster survivors, intended beneficiaries, and other stakeholders.

1.3 Qualifying Norms for Certification

Certification under the HAP Standard is open to organisations meeting the qualifying norms described below.

HAP Certification Qualifying Norms

1. Committed to provide humanitarian assistance on an impartial basis.

2. Formally declared as a not-for-profit organisation in the country or countries where it is legally registered and where it conducts humanitarian work.

3. Complies with the requirements for financial accountability under the law in the country or countries where it is legally registered and where it conducts humanitarian work.

4. Makes a publicly available statement of its humanitarian accountability framework.

1.4 Key Definitions

As the HAP Standard contains many references to accountability and quality, these terms and the related concepts of a humanitarian accountability framework, and a humanitarian quality management system are defined below.

Key Definitions

Accountability

Accountability is the means by which power is used responsibly. Humanitarian accountability involves taking account of, and accounting to disaster survivors.

Humanitarian Accountability Framework

A humanitarian accountability framework is a set of definitions, procedures, and standards that specify how an agency will ensure accountability to its stakeholders. It includes a statement of commitments, a baseline analysis of compliance, and an implementation policy, strategy, or plan. Commitments may include external standards, codes, principles, and guidelines, in addition to internal values, mandate, principles, charter, and guidelines. For HAP-certified agencies, this will include the HAP Principles of Accountability and the HAP Humanitarian Covenant.

Quality

Quality is the totality of features and characteristics of a product or service that makes it fit for the purpose of satisfying the stated or implied needs of the consumer or the intended beneficiary. Quality can be measured in terms of efficiency, effectiveness, outcome, and impact.

Quality Management System

A quality management system is a set of co-ordinated processes undertaken to continually improve the effectiveness and efficiency of an organisation in meeting the expectations of its customers. It comprises a documented quality policy, quality objectives, quality manual, and other documents needed to ensure the effective integration and implementation of the organisation's quality management processes.

Humanitarian Quality Management System

A humanitarian quality management system is a designated set of processes that enable continual improvement in an agency's performance in meeting the essential needs, and respecting the dignity, of disaster survivors.

2. The Humanitarian Accountability Covenant

2.1 Preamble

Recognising that the essence of humanitarian accountability is to respect the needs, concerns, capacities, and disposition of those we seek to assist, and to be answerable for our actions and decisions to interested parties, especially disaster survivors;

Respecting international humanitarian law, international refugee law, human rights law, and other relevant international treaties and national laws;

Reaffirming the primary duty of states to protect and assist people in times of armed conflict and calamity;

Acknowledging the duty of care regarding the well-being of intended beneficiaries incumbent upon all those engaging in humanitarian action;

Asserting the right of all in need to receive humanitarian assistance and protection on the basis of their informed consent;

Noting that operational constraints beyond our control can adversely affect our performance.

Agencies certified as compliant with the HAP Humanitarian Accountability and Quality Management Standard (2007) commit to being accountable for their actions and decisions in so far as these affect their humanitarian work, and in accordance with the principles for humanitarian action, additional declared interests, and quality management Benchmarks set out below.

2.2 Principles for Humanitarian Action

Agencies seeking to comply with the HAP Humanitarian Accountability and Quality Management Standard (2007) first commit themselves to accounting for their humanitarian work in relation to the general Principles for Humanitarian Action.

Principles for Humanitarian Action

Primary principles
- **Humanity:** upholding the right of all persons to receive and give assistance.
- **Impartiality:** providing humanitarian assistance in proportion to need and with respect to urgency, without discrimination based upon gender, age, race, impairment, ethnicity, and nationality or by political, religious, cultural, or organisational affiliation.

Secondary principles
- **Informed consent:** ensuring that the intended beneficiaries, or their representatives, understand and agree with the proposed humanitarian action and its implications.
- **Duty of care:** ensuring that humanitarian assistance meets or exceeds recognised minimum standards pertaining to the well-being of the intended beneficiaries.
- **Witness:** reporting on policies or practices that affect the well-being of disaster survivors.

Tertiary principles
- **Transparency:** ensuring that all relevant information is communicated to intended beneficiaries or their representatives, and other specified parties.
- **Independence:** acting under the authority of the governing body of the agency and in pursuit of the agency's mandate.
- **Neutrality:** refraining from giving material or political support to parties to an armed conflict.
- **Complementarity:** operating as a responsible member of the humanitarian assistance community.

2.3 Declaration of Additional Interests

Organisations that comply with the HAP Humanitarian Accountability and Quality Management Standard (2007) have declared additional affiliations, interests, values, and policies where these may have a direct bearing upon the well-being of disaster survivors and intended beneficiaries and the interests of specified stakeholders. These might include, but not be limited to:

- Gender policy
- Age-related policy
- Child protection policy
- Environmental policy
- Physical or mental impairment policy
- Conflict prevention and/or peace-building policy
- HIV and AIDS policy
- Technical specialisation
- Religious or political affiliations
- Conflict of interests policy

2.4 Humanitarian Quality Management Benchmarks

Organisations that comply with the HAP Humanitarian Accountability and Quality Management Standard (2007) can demonstrate that they meet specified performance benchmarks for:

1. Humanitarian quality management
2. Transparency
3. Beneficiary participation
4. Staff competencies
5. Complaints handling
6. Continual improvement

Under each Benchmark, the Standard defines requirements that must be met by the agency, with suggested means for verification of each.

Though not yet the subject of detailed requirements and performance indicators, organisations that comply with the HAP Humanitarian Accountability and Quality Management Standard (2007) will also pay due attention to:

1. Ensuring co-ordination and collaboration with other humanitarian actors

2. Committing to ethical fund-raising practices

3. Undertaking supply-chain management which considers local capacities and resources

2.5 Working with Humanitarian Partners

Aid agencies deliver humanitarian value in two different ways. *Operationally*, implementing projects directly through staff or volunteers; and *non-operationally*, providing financial, material, or technical support to a partner that implements projects directly through staff or volunteers. Some agencies combine both approaches. The HAP Humanitarian Accountability and Quality Management Standard (2007) applies to both operational and non-operational modes of humanitarian work.

Humanitarian Partnership Defined

A partnership is a relationship of mutual respect between two autonomous organisations that is founded upon a common purpose with defined expectations and responsibilities. Partnerships can be established with or without formal contractual agreements. Partners can be small community-based organisations or large national or international institutions. A humanitarian partnership is one in which two or more bodies agree to combine their resources to provide essential goods or services for disaster survivors.

Partnership in Practice

The diversity of humanitarian actors and the varied forms of humanitarian partnership demand flexibility in setting compliance norms for humanitarian partners. In some circumstances the best available humanitarian partners may not meet all technical standards of good practice, or may be unwilling or unable to comply with the certified agency's humanitarian accountability framework. In such cases, a certified agency will use the Principles of Humanitarian Action to justify a decision whether to support a partially compliant humanitarian actor. For example, a certified agency might support a humanitarian partner that is unable or unwilling to comply with a tertiary humanitarian principle, provided that the partner is especially well-placed to deliver humanitarian assistance that complies with the primary and secondary humanitarian principles.

Quality Partnerships

Quality partnerships are based upon trust and mutual respect. A partnership is undermined when one party tries to impose conditions upon the behaviour or activities of the other. Thus HAP Certification neither requires certified status from, nor confers certified status upon, the agency's humanitarian partners. Agencies committed to the HAP Standard may damage the quality of their humanitarian partnerships if they seek to impose the HAP Benchmarks upon a partner's management practices. However, good partnerships also entail mutual transparency and a commitment by both parties to the principle of continual improvement. Thus, HAP certified agencies shall at a minimum:

- explain their accountability and quality management obligations as HAP Standard bearers to their humanitarian partners;
- seek ways and means to improve the quality of the partnership with respect to the Principles of Accountability, and the Principles for Humanitarian Action.

3. Benchmarks for the HAP Standard

Benchmark 1:
The agency shall establish a humanitarian quality management system.

Benchmark 2:
The agency shall make the following information publicly available to intended beneficiaries, disaster-affected communities, agency staff, and other specified stakeholders: (a) organisational background; (b) humanitarian accountability framework; (c) humanitarian plan; (d) progress reports; and (e) complaints-handling procedures.

Benchmark 3:
The agency shall enable beneficiaries and their representatives to participate in programme decisions and seek their informed consent.

Benchmark 4:
The agency shall determine the competencies, attitudes, and development needs of staff required to implement its humanitarian quality management system.

Benchmark 5:
The agency shall establish and implement complaints-handling procedures that are effective, accessible, and safe for intended beneficiaries, disaster-affected communities, agency staff, humanitarian partners, and other specified bodies.

Benchmark 6:
The agency shall establish a process of continual improvement for its humanitarian accountability framework and humanitarian quality management system.

Benchmark 1

The agency shall establish a humanitarian quality management system

	Requirement		Means of verification
1.1	The agency shall document its humanitarian accountability framework referring to all relevant internal and external accountability and quality standards, codes, guidelines, and principles committed to by the agency	**1**	Review copy of documented humanitarian accountability framework and cross-reference with all relevant agency commitments including the agency's non-disclosure policy
		2	Verify that the document is made publicly accessible throughout the agency and to its humanitarian partners
		3	Review agency's strategy to support humanitarian partners in developing their capacity to comply with the Principles of Accountability and Principles for humanitarian action
1.2	The agency shall demonstrate that its humanitarian quality management system enables implementation of its humanitarian accountability framework	**1**	Confirm existence of and review implementation procedures for the humanitarian quality management system
		2	Interview humanitarian partners to confirm awareness of agency's humanitarian accountability framework

Benchmark 2

The agency shall make the following information publicly available to intended beneficiaries, disaster-affected communities, agency staff, and other specified stakeholders: (a) organisational background; (b) humanitarian accountability framework; (c) humanitarian plan; (d) progress reports; and (e) complaints handling procedures

	Requirement		Means of verification
2.1	The agency shall ensure that information is presented in languages, formats, and media that are accessible and comprehensible for beneficiaries and specified stakeholders *See definitions below*	1 2 3 4 5 6	Review how the languages, formats, and media have been determined Review documentation provided on organisational background, humanitarian accountability framework, humanitarian plan and financial summary, progress reports, and complaints-handling procedures Review guidelines for information dissemination Review information availability and accessibility Compare languages used by intended beneficiaries, local staff, and specified stakeholders with that used in documents provided Interview beneficiaries to verify information availability

Definitions:

Humanitarian Plan: To include overall goal and objectives (outputs/expected results), timeframe and linked financial summary.

Progress Reports: To include progress as measured against the humanitarian plan and financial summary. Reports to be made available at agreed intervals.

	Requirement		Means of verification
2.2	The agency shall inform disaster-affected communities about beneficiary selection criteria and deliverables as agreed with their representatives	**1**	Demonstrate that intended beneficiaries have been informed about selection criteria and entitlements, whether through minutes of meetings, letters of agreement, information boards, or other verifiable means
		2	Interview beneficiary representatives, beneficiaries, and agency personnel
2.3	The agency shall include its name and contact details in all publicly available information	**1**	Review contact details at appropriate and publicly accessible sites
2.4	The agency shall make available information about the relevant parts of its structure, including staff roles and responsibilities	**1**	Review availability and accessibility of information provided

Benchmark 3

The agency shall enable beneficiaries and their representatives to participate in programme decisions and seek their informed consent

	Requirement		Means of verification
3.1	The agency shall specify the processes it uses to identify intended beneficiaries and their representatives with specific reference to gender, age, disability, and other identifiable vulnerabilities	1	Review mechanism used to identify and disaggregate intended beneficiaries
		2	Review processes used to enable participation
		3	Interview staff about the processes for enabling participation
3.2	The agency shall enable intended beneficiaries and their representatives to participate in project design, implementation, monitoring, and evaluation	1	Demonstrate how its analysis of capacity has influenced implementation
		2	Review the appointment process of beneficiary representatives
		3	Review actual beneficiary input and impact on project design, implementation, monitoring, and evaluation
		4	Review the process used for establishing beneficiary criteria
		5	Review records of meetings held with beneficiary representatives

Benchmark 4

The agency shall determine the competencies, attitudes, and development needs of staff required to implement its humanitarian quality management system

	Requirement		Means of verification
4.1	The agency shall maintain a statement of the competencies (knowledge, skills, and behaviours) and attitudes required from its staff	1	Review job descriptions, recruitment files, and vacancy notices
		2	Interview agency staff responsible for recruitment, assignment, and training
4.2	The agency shall ensure that staff are aware of the humanitarian accountability framework and humanitarian quality management system, their relevance and importance, and that they understand their responsibilities in their implementation	1	Review induction and briefing procedures
		2	Interview staff to check awareness
4.3	The agency shall implement a system to review staff performance and competencies, including their knowledge, skills, behaviours, and attitudes	1	Review the performance management system
		2	Review performance appraisal documents and other formal approaches
		3	Review follow up activities
		4	Interview staff to check the impact of appraisal and performance management
4.4	The agency shall enable continual staff development for more effective implementation of the humanitarian quality management system	1	Review staff training records
		2	Review other staff development approaches
		3	Review agency support for the continual improvement of its humanitarian partners

Benchmark 5

The agency shall establish and implement complaints-handling procedures that are effective, accessible, and safe for intended beneficiaries, disaster-affected communities, agency staff, humanitarian partners, and other specified bodies

Requirement	Means of verification
5.1 The agency shall ask intended beneficiaries and the host community about appropriate ways to handle complaints	1 Demonstrate that findings from consultations have been incorporated into complaints-handling procedures
5.2 The agency shall establish and document complaints-handling procedures which clearly state: • the right of beneficiaries and other specified stake-holders to file a complaint • the purpose, parameters, and limitations of the procedure • the procedure for submitting complaints • the steps taken in processing complaints • confidentiality and non-retaliation policy for complainants • the process for safe referral of complaints that the agency is not equipped to handle • the right to receive a response	1 Review the documented procedures 2 Review samples of complaints to verify that complainants have been able to understand and use the procedure 3 Review budget, contracts, and support provided to humanitarian partners to implement this requirement 4 Interview field staff, affected community members, and/or intended beneficiaries about their perceptions and the adequacy of the procedures

	Requirement		Means of verification
5.3	The agency shall ensure that intended beneficiaries, affected communities, and its staff understand the complaints-handling procedures	1	Review strategy and activities for raising awareness among these groups of their right to file a complaint and the procedures to use
		2	Review documents about the complaints-handling procedures made available to intended beneficiaries
		3	Interview staff, affected community members, and/or intended beneficiaries to verify awareness of and adequacy of the procedures and confidence in their integrity
5.4	The agency shall verify that all complaints received are handled according to the stated procedures	1	Review a sample of both pending and processed complaints, to check the integrity of the system
		2	Review reports on the integrity of the complaints-handling process
5.5	The agency shall establish and implement an effective and safe complaints-handling mechanism for its staff, consistent with the requirements set out in 5.2	1	Review the procedure and samples of complaints made
		2	Interview staff to verify awareness of procedure and confidence in its integrity

Benchmark 6

The agency shall establish a process of continual improvement for its humanitarian accountability framework and humanitarian quality management system

Requirement	Means of verification
6.1 The agency shall specify the processes used for continual improvement of: • the agency's humanitarian accountability framework • the agency's humanitarian quality management system, inclusive of all HAP Benchmarks	**1** Review continual improvement process document/system **2** Note the dates when it was created and last updated **3** Dissemination: note if the latest version is accessible at all levels within the agency **4** Review meeting agendas and minutes to note discussions held and decisions taken to improve processes **5** Demonstrate how lessons learned impact current processes **6** Review feedback from governing bodies **7** Review internal and external audits and evaluations pertinent to the agency and how evaluation recommendations are acted upon and learning is incorporated
6.2 The agency shall together with its humanitarian partners monitor and evaluate the agreed means to improve the quality of the partnership with respect to the Principles of Accountability and the Principles for Humanitarian Action	**1** Review improvement plans (agreed actions, strategies for learning) for partners, noting date of drafting **2** Review monitoring and evaluation reports and note impact on improvement plan **3** Review partner contracts and note inclusion of relevant contractual support and expectations of both parties

Annex 2: Acronyms and glossary

Acronyms

ALNAP:	Accountability and Performance in Humanitarian Action
CARB:	Certification and Accreditation and Review and Board
CEO:	chief executive officer
ECB:	Emergency Capacity Building Project
ESC:	Editorial Steering Committee
HAF:	Humanitarian accountability framework
HAP:	Humanitarian Accountability Partnership
HQMS:	Humanitarian quality management system
ISO:	International Organization for Standardization
NGO:	non-government organisation
PDCA:	Plan–do–check–act quality assurance cycle
SGBV:	Sexual and gender-based violence
SWOT:	Strengths, weaknesses, opportunities, and threats (analytical tool)
UN:	United Nations

Glossary of terms used

Accountability: Accountability is the means by which power is used responsibly. Humanitarian accountability involves taking account of, and accounting to, disaster survivors.

Accreditation: Procedure by which an authoritative body (such as HAP) formally recognises that a body (e.g. network) or person (e.g. consultant) is competent to carry out a specific task that is certified.

Agency mandate: An agency's mandate or mission statement is a formal statement approved by its governance mechanisms that articulates the reason for its existence and the focus of its activity.

Analytical tools: Methods used to process and interpret information, e.g. SWOT analysis (which looks at strengths, weaknesses, opportunities, and threats).

Appraisal (1) performance: Process of reviewing a person's performance to determine the quality or quantity and value of their work outputs. Appraisals form part of a performance management system. They can be undertaken through self-assessment or through an interactive interview. Appraisal can be 'downward', 'upward', or '360 degrees'.

Appraisal (2) project: Process of designing a project intended to meet assessed needs and specific objectives.

Audit: An objective assessment of the way an organisation functions. It is a quality assurance activity designed to add value and improve an organisation's operations. Internal auditing can be carried out and is usually undertaken by a unit reporting to management. External auditing is conducted by an independent organisation.

Baseline study: An analysis describing the situation prior to an intervention, against which progress can be assessed or comparisons made.

Benchmark: Reference point or standard against which performance or achievements can be assessed. The HAP Standard comprises six benchmarks set as the agreed minimum achievement levels to ensure accountability to beneficiaries.

Beneficiary: The term 'beneficiary' refers to individuals, groups, or organisations who have been designated as the intended recipients of humanitarian assistance or protection in an aid intervention. In this Guide, the term 'beneficiary' is concerned with the contractual relationship between the aid agency and the persons whom the agency has undertaken to assist. The term has come under scrutiny, as in some cultures or contexts it may be interpreted negatively. Alternative suggestions are: people affected by disaster; the affected population; recipients of aid; claimants; clients (see also 'Disaster survivor').

Certification: The formal evaluation of an organisation against accepted criteria or standards, according to an established methodology used to measure and rate compliance and by an independent and recognised body.

Certification body: A third party which assesses and certifies compliance of a system with a specified standard, under the oversight and authorisation of an accreditation agency. The HAP Certification Board is the certification body of the HAP Standard.

Competencies: The combination of observable and measurable knowledge, skills, abilities, and personal attributes that contribute to enhanced employee performance and ultimately result in organisational success.

Complaint and feedback mechanisms: Mechanisms through which an organisation enables stakeholders to complain against its decisions or actions, and through which it ensures that these complaints are properly reviewed and acted upon. Enabling the community to complain or give feedback is an essential part of accountability and of protecting the right of those served by humanitarian organisations to have a say.

Confidentiality: An ethical and good practice principle that requires the protection of information shared within a service relationship.

An organisation that upholds confidentiality prohibits personnel from disclosing information about the people they interact with, unless they have given their written consent.

Consultation: The process of getting information from, or sharing it with, people who are affected by, or involved in a situation or process.

Corrective action procedures: Corrective actions are steps that are taken to remove the causes of an existing non-conformity or to make quality improvements. Corrective actions address actual problems. In general, the corrective action process can be thought of as a problem-solving process. After an audit has taken place, recommendations will be made on how to correct areas of non-compliance.

Corrective action request:

Major: A finding which highlights that the agency has not effectively implemented an element or requirement of the HAP Standard, to an extent that the ability to fulfil that element or requirement is absent, or that there has been a complete breakdown in the ability of the agency to meet that requirement. This constitutes a major non-conformity with the Standard.

Minor: A finding that an element or requirement of the HAP Standard is not being met, but not to the extent that the agency fails to effectively provide services in general compliance with the intent of the Standard. This constitutes a minor non-conformity with the Standard.

Cross-cutting issues: These are issues that have been identified as essential parts of humanitarian aid. They should be included in all programmes. Examples of cross-cutting issues include protection, gender equality, children, older people, disabled people, effects on the environment.

Disaster: A calamitous event resulting in loss of life, great human suffering and distress, and large-scale material damage. It can be man-made (war, conflict, terrorist acts, etc.) or it can have natural causes (drought, flood, earthquake, etc.).

Disaster survivor: HAP uses the term 'disaster survivor' to refer to all living persons who have been directly affected by armed conflict or by other calamitous events. Disaster survivors are not always necessarily beneficiaries (see 'Beneficiary' above).

Equality: Having the same rights and status, being equal or balanced. Gender equality, for example, is about promoting equality between women and men in all aspects of development work. It is about giving people the opportunity to build a better life for themselves, their families, and their communities. It helps in the following ways: it supports a more accurate understanding of the situation; it facilitates the design of more appropriate responses; it highlights opportunities and resources; it draws attention to issues of power; it provides a link between humanitarian assistance and longer-term development assistance (from: CIDA, *Gender Equality and Humanitarian Assistance Guide*: www.acdicida.gc.ca/INET/IMAGES.NSF/vLUImages /Africa/$file/Guide-Gender.pdf).

Evaluation: The systematic and objective assessment of an ongoing or completed project, programme, or policy, looking at its design, implementation, and results.

Feedback: The transmission of findings generated through the evaluation process to parties for whom it is relevant and useful, so as to facilitate learning.

Finding: A finding is a conclusion arrived at on the basis of assessment and an analysis of the evidence. During an audit the auditor will report on a number of findings, explaining how an agency meets a requirement/benchmark.

Framework: An essential supporting structure; a basic system.

Gender: The term refers to the social differences between males and females that are learned and, though deeply rooted in every culture, are changeable over time and have wide variations both within and between cultures. 'Gender' determines the roles, responsibilities, privileges, expectations, and limitations for males and females in any culture (from: Inter-Agency Standing Committee (IASC) (2005), *Guidelines for Gender-based Violence Interventions in Humanitarian Settings,* www.humanitarianinfo.org/iasc)

Gender-based violence: An umbrella term for any harmful act that is perpetrated against a person's will, and that is based in socially ascribed (gender) differences between males and females. The term 'gender-based violence' is often used interchangeably with the term 'violence against women', but men and boys may also be victims of gender-based violence, especially sexual violence (IASC).

Gender analysis: An exploration of the relationships of women and men in society, and the unequal power in these relationships. It brings the inequalities to the surface and to the attention of people who can make a difference.

Good practices: successful approaches adopted by other organisations or individuals and shared within the sector.

Humanitarian accountability framework: A humanitarian accountability framework is a set of definitions, procedures, and standards that specify how an agency will ensure accountability to its stakeholders. It includes a statement of commitments, a baseline analysis of compliance and an implementation policy, strategy, or plan. Commitments may include external standards, codes, principles, and guidelines, in addition to internal values, mandate, principles, charter, and guidelines. For HAP-certified agencies, this will include the HAP Principles of Accountability and the HAP Humanitarian Covenant.

Impact: Positive and negative, primary and secondary long-term effects produced by an intervention, directly or indirectly, intended or unintended.

Impartiality: An approach to the provision of humanitarian assistance and services which is non-discriminatory, proportionate to needs, and free of subjective distinction. A guiding principle of organisations claiming to be humanitarian. In the HAP Standard, impartiality is defined as: 'the provision of humanitarian assistance on the basis of need alone, without discrimination based upon race, ethnicity, and nationality or by political, religious, cultural, or organisational affiliation'.

Indicator: Quantitative or qualitative factor or variable that provides a simple and reliable means to measure achievement, to reflect the changes connected to an intervention, or to help assess the performance of a development actor. Quantitative indicators use numbers, while qualitative indicators use words or pictures. Both types of indicator are necessary. For example, a quantitative indicator may show the number of children receiving rations; a qualitative indicator can show how satisfied they are with the food (from: ECB, *Impact Measurement and Accountability in Emergencies: The Good Enough Guide*, Tool 10, p.29).

Job description: Explicit obligations and specific tasks required of personnel as a condition of employment. Such descriptions are set out in writing and may include educational, experience, and skill requirements associated with the job.

Lessons learned: Generalisations based on evaluation experiences with projects, programmes, or policies that abstract from the specific circumstances to broader situations.

Monitoring: This is a continuous process that takes place throughout the timeframe of a project. A continuing function by which data about specified indicators are collected systematically and provided to management and to the main stakeholders of an ongoing development intervention. The data indicate the extent of progress, the achievement of objectives, and how allocated funds are being used.

Neutrality: Refers to the principle that to enjoy the confidence of all, an organisation may not take sides in hostilities or engage at any time in controversies of a political, racial, religious, or ideological nature. In the HAP Standard, this is defined as 'refraining from giving material or political support to parties to armed conflict'.

NGO: NGOs (non-government organisations) are organisations, both national and international, which are constituted separate from the government of the country in which they are founded.

Organisational structure: The structure of an organisation is the pattern of responsibilities, authorities, and relationships that control how people perform their functions and govern how they interact with one another.

Participation: Participation in humanitarian action is understood as the engagement of affected populations in one or more phases of the project cycle: assessment, design, implementation, monitoring, and evaluation. This engagement can take a variety of forms. Far more than a set of tools, participation is first and foremost a state of mind that places members of affected populations at the heart of humanitarian action as social actors, with insights on their situation and with competencies, energy, and ideas of their own (from: ALNAP, *Participation by Crisis-Affected Populations: A Guide Book for Practitioners*).

Participatory evaluation: Evaluation method in which representatives of agencies and stakeholders (including beneficiaries) work together in designing, carrying out, and interpreting an evaluation. This forms part of the requirements for Benchmark 3 of the HAP Standard, as it will strongly support transparency and accountability.

Partners: The individuals and organisations that collaborate to achieve mutually agreed objectives.

Performance: The degree to which an intervention, or a partner, operates according to specific criteria, standards, or guidelines, or achieves results in accordance with stated goals or plans.

Performance improvement: Increasing the impact of an organisation in fulfilling its aims and objectives, for the maximum benefit of its users or members, and for its cause.

Policies: Written statements of principles and positions that guide organisational operations and services.

Practice: Established actions or ways of proceeding in the regular performance of organisational duties. Policies and procedures often guide practice.

Preventative actions: Preventative actions are steps that are taken to remove the causes of potential non-conformities or to make quality improvements. Preventative actions address potential problems, i.e. ones that have not yet occurred. In general, the preventative action process can be thought of as a risk analysis process.

Principle: A fundamental truth or law as a basis for reasoning or action; a personal or corporate code of conduct. The HAP Principles of Accountability form the basis of the HAP Standard.

Procedures: The designated methods by which broad policies are implemented and organisational operations are carried out. Procedures are usually contained in writing in an operating or programme manual, as an adjunct to board-approved policies.

Process evaluation: An evaluation of the internal dynamics of implementing organisations, their policy instruments, their service delivery mechanisms, their management practices, and the linkages among these. This is an evaluation of the way an organisation carries out its work rather than an impact evaluation of its net effect.

Protection: 'Activities aimed at obtaining full respect for the rights of the individual in accordance with the letter and the spirit of the relevant bodies of law (i.e. human rights, humanitarian and refugee law) … [which are] conduct[ed] impartially and not on the basis of race, national or ethnic origin, language or gender.' * Protection of the right of beneficiaries to have a say, and the duty of agencies to respond, is a key driving factor for the HAP Standard.

Quality: The totality of features and characteristics of a product or service that bear on its ability to satisfy stated or implied needs. It can be seen as a measure of excellence.

---

* C. von Flüe and J. de Maio (1999) 'Third Workshop on Protection for Human Rights and Humanitarian Organizations', A Report of the Workshop held at the International Committee of the Red Cross, 18–20 January, Geneva.

Quality assurance: Quality assurance is defined as a set of activities whose purpose is to demonstrate that an entity meets all quality requirements. Quality assurance activities are carried out in order to inspire the confidence of both 'customers' and managers, i.e. confidence that all quality requirements are being met. Examples of quality assurance activities include staff appraisals, reviews during implementation, evaluations, etc.

Quality management: The co-ordinated activities used to direct and control an agency with regards to quality and quality assurance.

Recommendations: Proposals aimed at enhancing the effectiveness, quality, or efficiency of a development intervention; at redesigning its objectives; and/or at the reallocation of resources.

Relevance: The extent to which the objectives of a development intervention are consistent with beneficiary requirements, country needs, global priorities, and partners' and donors' policies.

Results: The output, outcome, or impact (intended or unintended, positive or negative) of a development intervention.

Risk analysis: An analysis or an assessment of factors (could be called assumptions) that affect or are likely to affect the successful achievement of an intervention's objectives. The Logical Framework (log frame) planning method enables users to track changes aimed at (goals, objectives) and achieved (outputs, outcomes, impacts) in relation to the activities undertaken. A detailed examination of the potential unwanted and negative consequences to human life, health, property, or the environment posed by interventions.

Sexual abuse and exploitation: Sexual abuse is the actual or threatened intrusion of a sexual nature, whether by force or under unequal or coercive conditions. Sexual exploitation is any actual or attempted abuse of a position of vulnerability, differential power, or trust for sexual purposes, including, but not limited to, profiting monetarily, socially, or politically from the sexual exploitation of another (IASC).

Stakeholders: Agencies, organisations, groups, or individuals who have a direct or indirect interest in the development of an intervention or its evaluation.

Standard: A quality or measure serving as a basis, example, or principle to which others should conform or by which others are judged. A required or specified level of excellence.

Surveillance: This refers to the period of HAP accreditation or certification, when semi-annual audits and report reviews take place to verify that compliance with the Standard is ongoing.

Terms of reference: Written document presenting the purpose and scope of a specific piece of work, e.g. evaluation, the methods to be used, the standard against which performance is to be assessed or analyses are to be conducted, the resources and time allocated, reporting requirements.

Transparency: The provision of accessible and timely information to stakeholders and the opening up of organisational procedures, structures, and processes to their assessment.

Validation: Confirmation by examination and provision of objective evidence that the particular requirements for a specific intended use can be consistently fulfilled.

Annex 3: Tools

The tools contained in this section are practical guidelines and tips aimed at providing further guidance for agencies interested in strengthening their accountability systems. The Benchmark sections of the Guide provide 'best practice' advice and recommend a number of tools of particular relevance to the issue under discussion. The tools are therefore designed to be used in conjunction with the Benchmark sections, but may also be used separately from them. Some of the tools, on stakeholder consultations or performance assessment, for example, may be of general use to project managers in their day-to-day work, irrespective of whether they are involved in the HAP Certification process or not.

As well as original materials developed by HAP itself (Tools 6, 7, 17–21, and 25–27), this section reproduces resources produced by other organisations and initiatives concerned with accountability issues, namely World Vision International (Tools 8, 9, 22, 23, and 28) and the Emergency Capacity Building Project (Tools 1–5, 10–16, 24, and 29); these are credited accordingly.

The Emergency Capacity Building Project (ECB)'s *Good Enough Guide* offers practical wisdom for the busy field worker on how to be accountable to local people and how to measure programme impact in an emergency. The 'good enough' approach favours simple solutions over elaborate ones and encourages the user to choose tools that are safe, essential, quick, and simple to implement.

The ECB guide suggests some basic, tried, and tested methods for putting impact measurement and accountability into practice from the beginning of a project. It is aimed at humanitarian practitioners, project officers, and managers with some experience in the field, and draws on the work of field staff, NGOs, and inter-agency initiatives, including HAP International. Although written with an emergency setting in mind, the guide can also be used in the context of longer-term 'development' programming. The original ECB tool numbers are included in parentheses in the copyright line of the tool, for easy reference (Emergency Capacity Building Project (2007) *Impact Measurement and Accountability in Emergencies. The Good Enough Guide*, Oxfam Publishing, Oxford, UK).

Tool 1
How accountable are you? Checking public information

This tool can help you check whether you are providing people affected by the emergency with basic information about your agency and the project. By asking people what information they have received, you can check how they see you and whether you are providing the information they need at the right time and in the right way.

This tool can be used at different stages during the project: at the start to help you explain who you are and what your agency can do (see also Tool 10 [ECB Tool 1]); after significant changes, for example, if the level of food ration is cut; and at the end of a project as part of your exit strategy.

For field team members

Have you provided the checklist information (opposite) to beneficiaries and their representatives in an accessible way?

For people affected by an emergency

Have you received the checklist information (opposite) from project staff?

Checklist

	Basic information	Yes	No
1	Background information about the NGO		
2	Details of the current project		
3	Project contact information		
	Reports on project implementation		
4	Regular reports on project performance		
5	Regular financial reports		
6	Information about significant project changes		
	Opportunities for involvement		
7	Dates and locations of key participation events		
8	Specific contact details for making comments or suggestions		
9	Details of how to make complaints about the NGO's activities		

From: A. Jacobs (2005) 'Accountability to Beneficiaries: A Practical Checklist', draft, Mango for Oxfam GB (adapted). **(ECB Tool 2)**

Tool 2
How to decide whether to do a survey

Surveys can be used to collect information from large numbers of people before, during, or after a project. Surveys are useful tools but can be complex and resource-intensive in practice. Before deciding if you are ready to conduct a survey, think about some of the advantages and disadvantages.

Surveys: some advantages and disadvantages

Advantages	Disadvantages
A survey can provide specific information about a lot of people in a short time.	Only a short time can be spent with each person so the information you receive about them may be limited.
	You will also need time to analyse and use all the information collected.
Information from some of the people can be used to make plans for all the population.	The people selected may be easy to get to or willing to co-operate, but not necessarily representative of the population.
The methods and forms used to collect information must be standardised so that results can be reliably compared (for example, see Tool 3 [ECB Tool 8]).	These methods may produce superficial information.Interviewees may give the answers they think you want to hear.
A survey requires careful consideration beforehand in order to determine what information can be obtained, from whom, how, and when.	Time may be scarce. If people's way of life is not fully understood then the information they provide may prove misleading.
A large amount of information can be obtained cheaply if unpaid or volunteer staff are used.	A large-scale survey is often difficult to supervise because of staff costs and distances to be covered.

From: Partners in Evaluation: Evaluating Development and Community Programmes with Participants, © *Marie-Thérèse Feuerstein 1986. Reproduced by permission of Macmillan Publishers Ltd.* **(ECB Tool 7)**

Tool 3
How to assess child-protection needs

This basic checklist can be used in the different areas in which you work or plan to work. It can be further adapted to assess protection needs for other vulnerable groups too.

1. Are there any reported cases of children:
    *   killed in this disaster
    *   injured
    *   missing?

2. Are there groups of children without access to:
    *   food
    *   water
    *   shelter
    *   health care
    *   education?

3. Have these cases been reported? To which organisation?

4. Are there any reported cases of:
    *   separated children
    *   families with missing children
    *   children sent away to safe places?

5. Have families generally moved as a group?

6. Are there groups of children living together without adults? Do they include children less than five years of age?

7. Are there individual adults who have assumed care responsibility for a large group of children?

8. List any organisations taking care of separated children.

9. Are there other serious protection and care concerns for girls not already identified above?

10. Are there other serious protection and care concerns for boys not already identified above?

11. Which organisations are working on child-protection issues in the area?

From: World Vision 'Rapid child protection assessment form in situations of natural disasters', (internal, adapted). **(ECB Tool 8)**

Tool 4
How to start using indicators

Your agency may have its own approach to indicators. If not, this introduction can help you start to develop 'good enough' indicators with people affected by an emergency.

Indicators are numbers or statements that help measure, simplify, and communicate changes and impact.

Quantitative indicators use numbers, while qualitative indicators use words or pictures. Both types of indicator are necessary. For example, a quantitative indicator may tell you the number of children receiving rations: a qualitative indicator can tell you how satisfied they are with the food.

Use the 'good enough' approach when thinking about indicators:

- Find out if the project already has some indicators.
- Don't develop too many new ones: use as few as possible.
- Try to have a balance of quantitative and qualitative indicators.
- Collect only the information you need most.
- Check that a preferred indicator really will measure the change desired.
- After using your indicators to track changes, analyse and use this information in decision-making.

Sphere indicators

The 'good enough' approach recognises the need to refer to widely accepted standards. Sphere provides the best-known indicators of humanitarian impact: they create a 'common language' and enable comparison between projects.

Sphere acknowledges that indicators may be modified in certain contexts. In the case below, an agency explains why it could not deliver the recommended 7–15 litres of water per person per day. When indicators cannot be met, it is important to be transparent, to record reasons during assessment and impact monitoring and, if possible, to advocate so that indicators can be met.

160

Ethiopia project

'In a drought project in Ethiopia in 2000 we delivered water to over 400,000 people. We delivered approximately 5 litres per person per day instead of the recommended 15 litres. That was beyond donor and logistical capacities. We clearly stated that we were delivering water only for consumption and cooking.'

Indicators of change

Wherever possible, involve women, men, and children affected by the emergency in deciding the changes they want to see. Ask community members at a meeting, workshop, or in individual discussion about what they hope to see when the project has been completed. Hold separate meetings for women and for other groups.

Ask people affected about what will happen if the project is a success. 'Imagine the project is finished. How will people benefit? How will it affect your life? What will you see happening?' People's responses to these questions help give you the indicators you need to track progress and change.

Indicators of change developed by a community:

- May or may not be compatible with other indicators
- May seem illogical to outsiders
- May not be applicable in other emergencies or other communities
- May not be time-bound
- May not enable comparison between projects.

However, they are a way of making sure that project staff look at the situation through the eyes of beneficiaries, enable people to express their views, and take into account their experiences and wishes.

Sudan project

In a water project in south Sudan, project staff gauged success using a Sphere indicator that measured the distance of the water point from the community.

But in the same project the community measured success by counting the number of girls going to school. When the water point was nearer the community, the girls took their buckets to school and picked up the water on their way home.

How did people feel about the changes in their community as a result of the water supply close by and the fact that girls could go to school? [See *The Good Enough Guide*, page 23, for an example of how to measure satisfaction.]

From: V. M. Walden (2005) *'Community Indicators'*, Oxfam (internal); L. Bishop (2002) *'First steps in Monitoring and Evaluation'*, Charities Evaluation Services; interview with Margarita Clark, Save the Children. **(ECB Tool 10)**

Tool 5
How to give a verbal report

Even when people affected by the emergency have participated throughout the project, some people will know more about it than others. Here are some tips for giving a verbal report about the project to the community in general.

Keep it short

Don't hide information but aim to help people remember the main points about what has happened.

Think what people need to know

Prepare a verbal presentation that suits people's needs.

Emphasise key points

If you can, use posters, quotes, photos, slides, tables, and charts.

Encourage participation

A question and answer session, a panel, or a short play can help.

Encourage people to say what they think

People may have conflicting views of the project and the changes it is making. Think ahead about how you will deal with these different views.

Listen and be tactful

Try to maintain a good atmosphere and good relationships between people, especially if they express different views. Try to end the discussion on a positive note.

From: Partners in Evaluation: Evaluating Development and Community Programmes with Participants, © Marie-Thérèse Feuerstein 1986. Reproduced by permission of Macmillan Publishers Ltd. **(ECB Tool 13)**

Tool 6
Plan–do–check–act quality assurance cycle (PDCA)

The PDCA cycle was originally conceived by Walter Shewhart in the 1930s; it was later adopted by W. Edwards Deming and has thus become known as the Deming Cycle, or Deming Wheel. The model provides a framework for the improvement of a process or system. It can be used to guide the entire continual improvement plan, or to develop specific action plans once results from evaluations, lessons learned, and improvement recommendations have been identified.

The PDCA cycle is designed to be never-ending, capturing the spirit of continual quality improvement. It establishes a flow that links one stage to the next and then restarts the analysis over again. (Note: In development aid, the PDCA cycle is sometimes adapted to plan, do, evaluate (monitor), improve.)

Plan: an improvement, a change, a corrective or preventative action which is aimed at improving your agency's overall quality, effectiveness, and efficiency. Key steps in this phase:

• Analyse what you intend to improve – you can use a SWOT (strengths, weaknesses, opportunities, and threats) approach.

• Design your implementation plan.

• Put in place the resources you will need (staff, time, finance).

Do: implement your plan. Key step in this phase:

• Make sure that you have included a mechanism for capturing impact/feedback.

Check: monitor and evaluate the results achieved from the implementation. Ascertain what went right and what went wrong. Key steps in this phase:

• It is important to monitor if the plan is working well in both the short and the long term.

• Ask whether the plan is really having the impact and bringing about the improvement intended.

• In order to do this, some progress indicators and impact objectives will be helpful.

Act: decision time: adopt the changes, further develop, or discard. Key steps/questions to ask in this phase:

- Did the changes suggested take too much time to implement?
- Was the plan difficult to follow or keep to?
- Was it cost-effective?
- Did it add the expected value?
- Make the decision to continue, which could involve further improvement and expansion.

This now takes you back to **Plan.**

This is a commonly used method of evaluating all or part of a quality management system.

Below is an example of a checklist which indicates the steps involved in an improvement cycle.

Step	Activity	Check
1	Identify a process or procedure that needs to be improved/reviewed.	
2	Select a team that knows the process/procedure.	
3	Collate and clarify knowledge of the process/procedure (includes data collection, needs analysis, flowcharting process, etc.).	
4	Assess and establish the underlying causes of the problem and why there has been poor quality or variation in performance.	
5	Work through the PDCA cycle using the changes suggested.	

© *HAP International*

Tool 7
SWOT analysis (strengths, weaknesses, opportunities, and threats)

The SWOT tool helps to analyse an agency's current status, and explore ways ahead.

	Internal Related to the internal aspects of the agency (all levels)	**External** Related to the operational environment the agency works in (international, regional, and national)
Positive	***Strengths*** e.g. related to: • Information provision • Beneficiary participation • Local capacity mapping • Staff performance appraisal • Complaints-handling feed-back	***Opportunities*** e.g. related to: • Sustainability of projects • Beneficiary partnerships • Improved co-ordination
Negative	***Weaknesses*** e.g. related to: • Translation of information • Beneficiary access	***Threats*** e.g. related to: • Insecurity • Dissatisfied community

© *HAP International*

165

Tool 8
Community engagement: stakeholder analysis

What is a stakeholder analysis?

Stakeholder analysis is the identification of a project's key stakeholders, an assessment of their interests, and of the ways in which those interests affect a project. There is no 'one way' of doing a stakeholder analysis. The key element is deciding what kind of analysis is needed for what purpose.

Purpose of stakeholder analysis:

- To identify people and groups with an interest in a project.
- To better understand their interests, needs, and capabilities in relation to planning, monitoring, review, and evaluation.
- To understand the needs and interests of those not directly affected by an activity.
- To assess which groups can be directly involved at different stages of an activity.
- To identify potential synergies and obstacles with different groups and individuals.
- To inform development of future strategies.

Who are the stakeholders?

Stakeholders are people affected either positively or negatively by the project, directly or indirectly. For example:

- People affected by the impact of a project or activity
- People who can influence the project
- Individuals, groups, or institutions with interests in a project/programme
- Community groups, civil societies, organisations, financial sponsors, wider public, and external service providers.

Carrying out a stakeholder analysis

There are different ways to approach a stakeholder analysis, depending on its particular purpose and the type of analysis required. The example given here can be useful in assessing the importance of each stakeholder to the project.

This analysis involves the following steps:

1. Identify all individuals, groups, and organisations affected by the issues that the project seeks to address (this can be done by brainstorming in a group).

2. Categorise stakeholders according to interest groups, gender, individual status, ethnic affiliation, organisational affiliation, authority, power, etc.

3. Discuss whose interests are to be prioritised in relation to specific problems.

4. Identify the potential (strengths, weakness, opportunities, and threats) that each group has for coping with the issues addressed by the project.

5. Identify the linkages between stakeholders (conflicts of interest, co-operative relations, dependencies, and opportunities for better co-operation in project activities).

The table below indicates a framework for approaching a stakeholder analysis.

Stakeholders	Problems	Potentials	Linkages

References
Gosling, L. and M. Edwards (2003) *Toolkits: A practical guide to planning, monitoring, evaluation and impact assessment,* Save the Children UK.
Qualman, A. (1995) *Guidance Note on How to Do Stakeholder Analysis of Aid Projects and Programmes,* CIDA.
From: *Community Engagement & Accountability Workshop,* developed by Joshua Pepall, Humanitarian Accountability Team, World Vision, LTRT Sri Lanka, 2006. ©World Vision International - tool has been adapted.

Tool 9
Community programmes calendar

The community programmes calendar is designed to be used in a small group setting. Its purpose is to help project staff communicate programme plans to beneficiaries and other stakeholders, and to involve communities in decisions that affect their lives. It is a two-way process: the agency informs the community what kinds of activities they plan to undertake when, and the community provides information to the agency about different events during the calendar year which might affect those plans. During the discussion, the community will also learn how they can be involved throughout the programme cycle – from start to exit.

This tool is particularly useful because it uses symbols instead of words, which means that poor and illiterate people, who are often excluded from such planning discussions, can be included. It should not be seen as a one-off consultative participatory exercise, but rather as the start of a continuous process of dialogue between stakeholders and the agency, which should continue throughout the programme cycle. It can be used for:

- Community-level project or programme planning
- Risk assessment and management
- Community engagement planning (participation, information provision, information gathering, and consultation)
- Discussions around monitoring and evaluation.

Programmes calendar being used by LTRT HAT staff during a community meeting
© *Viraj Wahalatantri/World Vision 2007*

168

Stakeholder analysis

A stakeholder analysis should be completed before using the calendar. A stakeholder analysis is useful for mapping and identify projects, key stakeholders, their interests, and the ways in which those interests affect the project. Once such an analysis has been completed, it will become clearer which groups to involve in the community programmes calendar. Some of the audiences to consider using the tool with include:

- Community groups
- Government and authorities
- Agency staff
- Children's groups
- Other international NGOs, local NGOs, etc.
- Community mobilisers.

Calendar toolkit

All the items needed are included in this tool. The kit has been put together to make it as easy and manageable for field staff as possible. It includes the following items:

- 1 x programmes calendar
- 5 x season symbols (Islamic, Christian, Buddhist, monsoon, harvest)
- 6 x sector symbols (water/sanitation, housing/infrastructure, civil society, health/nutrition, child protection, economic recovery).

The calendar

The calendar should be printed or drawn to A1 scale (594 x 841 mm). If you don't have access to printers, use flip charts or tape together some sheets of A4 paper. Alternatively, draw a calendar on the ground. Write the names of the months, in the local language, across the top of the calendar (so that there is a column for each month). This row in which you write the month names needs to be quite deep, so that there is room to stick some season symbols in it without obscuring the month names. On the extreme left of the calendar (i.e. not in any of the month columns), stick symbols for each of the sectors in which you are planning to do some work in that community.

Community programmes calendar											
Jan	Feb	March	April	May	June	July	August	Sept	Oct	Nov	Dec

© Joshua Pepall/World Vision 2007

Season and sector symbols

Symbols representing religious festivals and seasons, and common sectors that agencies work in, are included at the end of this tool, for photocopying (or printing from the CD-ROM). They should be stuck on to the calendar with a removable adhesive, such as double-sided tape or masking tape. Be adaptable and creative. If you need to add another symbol not included here, ask a participant to select a stone, leaf, twig, or some other readily available object and use that.

How to use the calendar

1. Find a large open space. The calendar can be spread out on the ground, hung on a tree, or stuck on a wall.

2. Explain the purpose of the meeting: to provide information on activities, find out local information relating to seasonal events, answer questions, and discuss how stakeholders can be involved throughout the programme cycle. Briefly explain the sector symbols on the left-hand side.

3. Answer any questions about the process before you move on. If people have specific questions about activities, have the facilitator record them on a separate sheet and explain that they will be answered during the process. At the end of the

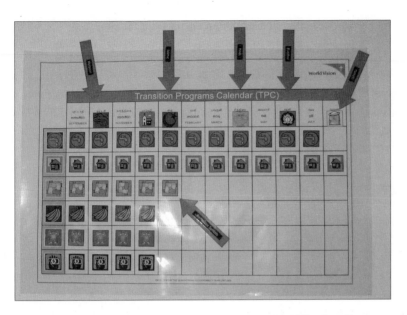

Programme calendar on display at the World Vision Sri Lanka Tsunami Relief Office, for staff comment and feedback on its development
© Joshua Pepall/World Vision 2007

session, have the facilitator review the question sheet and refer any unanswered questions to the appropriate sector co-ordinator.

4. Ask the community about seasonal patterns. For example, ask when the rainy season is, and then stick the monsoon symbol at the top of the calendar by the relevant month (without obscuring the name of the month).

5. Ask group members to stick the relevant religious festival symbols by the months in which they occur.

6. Next, briefly explain the kinds of activities the agency wishes to carry out within each sector, and when you plan to do them. Ask group members to stick the relevant sector symbols on the calendar in the columns for the months in which those activities will take place.

7. As you work your way through the different activities, remember the following:

   • Discuss with the group how they would like to be informed of project activities and progress.

171

- Clarify the aim of the programme and discuss what the activities are, your agency's responsibilities, and the responsibilities of the community as the project goes through its cycle.

- Use the meeting as an opportunity to gather information on community-based organisations or national organisations working in the area or sector. Make a list so that they can be assessed as possible partners.

- Provide participants with the criteria and entitlements for services.

- Discuss a suitable complaints-handling system.

- Brainstorm opportunities for community participation at each stage of the programme cycle.

- Encourage the group to discuss any problems with the planned activities, and possible solutions.

- Organise a community meeting schedule.

- Refer specific questions to the appropriate sector co-ordinator

8. At the end of the session provide your office contact details, answer outstanding participant questions, and address any misconceptions. Provide feedback to the relevant sector co-ordinators and district managers.

Season symbols

Harvest

Christian festival

Monsoon

Buddhist festival

Islamic festival

Sector symbols

Water and sanitation

Child protection

Housing and infrastructure

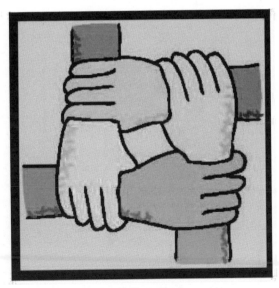

Civil society

177

Health and nutrition

Economic recovery

© *World Vision/Joshua Pepall (Humanitarian Accountability Advisor) World Vision Sri Lanka – tool has been adapted.*

Tool 10
How to introduce your agency: a need-to-know checklist

This checklist can be used to help make sure that field staff know the answers to questions they are likely to be asked by beneficiaries, government officials, and others. You can use it at the start of a project or in conjunction with Tool 29 [ECB Tool 11]) to brief new staff.

Who are we?

1. What is an NGO?
2. What is our mandate?
3. Why is our agency here?
4. Where do we get the money?

Our aim

5. What can we do for people affected by the emergency in relation to:
   a) Water and sanitation
   b) Shelter
   c) Livelihoods
   d) Public health promotion
   e) Other kinds of project?
6. Why do we do this rather than other things?

The project and the community

7. What is our project area?
8. Who decided?
9. Who was involved in deciding project activities?
10. What is the plan for the whole project?
11. How long will it last?
12. Who are the beneficiaries?
13. Why were some people chosen and not others?
14. Who was involved in deciding who the beneficiaries should be?
15. How does the project work? How are beneficiaries involved?
16. What will beneficiaries contribute?

17. What will we contribute?
18. What do the materials cost us?
19. What is the progress this month? What is the plan for next month?
20. What are the main challenges for technical staff this month?
21. What are technical staff doing to address these challenges?
22. What exactly will beneficiaries receive?
23. When will they receive it?

Dealing with problems or complaints

(See also Tool 5 [ECB Tool 13])

24. If something goes wrong with the project, what can people do?
25. If there is a problem with a community leader or community member working with us, what can people do?
26. If there is a problem with one of our staff (e.g. corruption, fraud, bad behaviour), what can people do?

Other organisations and the government

27. Which other NGOs are working in the project location?
28. What do they do?
29. What government assistance is available? How do people access it?
30. What other problems are people having? (e.g. being displaced, no access to land, not being able to meet government officials to resolve problems.)

From: T. Gorgonio and A. Miller (2005) 'Need To Know List', Oxfam GB (internal, adapted). **(ECB Tool 1)**

Tool 11
How to profile the affected community and assess initial needs

This tool can help you profile an affected community. It can be used in conjunction with Tool 12 (ECB Tool 5) and Tool 15 (ECB Tool 6) and can be repeated as the situation changes.

Suggested questions

1. What is the background of the affected group(s)? Are they from an urban or rural background?

2. What is the approximate number of people affected and their demographic characteristics? (Include a breakdown of the population by sex, and children under five. Include numbers of 5–14-year-olds, pregnant and lactating women, and those aged 60 and over, if data are available.)

3. Who are the marginalised/separated people in this population group (e.g. female-headed households, unaccompanied children, disabled, sick, elderly people, ethnic minorities, etc.). Do they have specific needs? How have they been affected by the current crisis?

4. Are there particular family, ethnic, religious, or other groupings among the affected people? Are any groups particularly hard to access?

5. Who are the key people to contact/consult? Are there any community members or elders leading the people affected by the emergency? Are there organisations with local expertise (e.g. churches, mosques, or local NGOs) that can be part of decision-making?

6. What are the biggest risks, in terms of health and protection against violence, faced by the various groups of people affected by this emergency, and what agency is addressing them?

How have women been affected? Do they have specific needs?

'In the early stages in Gujarat our distribution teams were almost exclusively male. The Sphere guidelines* prompted us to send an all-female survey team into earthquake-affected communities to talk to women. As a result, we developed a hygiene kit for women and got funding for 23,000 kits.'

'The immediate relief operations in Sri Lanka were largely gender-blind. Few organisations considered providing women with sanitary needs, underwear, or culturally appropriate clothing. The needs of pregnant or breastfeeding mothers were not sufficiently catered for.'

* Minimum standards
Sources: Srodecki (2001); IFRC (2005)

From: Oxfam (no date) 'Background Information: Checklist for Rapid Assessments In Emergencies' (adapted); IFRC (2000) Disaster Preparedness Training Manual (adapted); IFRC (2005) World Disasters Report 2005 (adapted); J. Srodecki (2001) 'World Vision use of Sphere standards in a large scale emergency: a case study of the spring 2001 Gujarat response', World Vision (internal, adapted). ***(ECB Tool 4)***

Tool 12
How to conduct an individual interview

Individual interviews can be used during assessments or surveys. An individual interview can mean a ten-minute conversation during an informal visit or a longer and more structured discussion, using a series of questions on a particular topic. Whatever the case, focus on essential information and build your interview around current concerns, e.g. profiling and needs assessment, tracking changes, or seeking feedback.

Aim to interview people at times that are safe and convenient for both staff and interviewees. The time your interviewee has available should determine how long your interview lasts. Make sure that people understand why you wish to talk to them and what you will do with the information they share. Never use people's names when using information without their express permission or that of their guardian.

Start with questions that are factual and relatively straightforward to answer. Move on to more sensitive issues, if necessary, only when the person you are interviewing is more at ease.

Make sure people know that you value their time and participation. Don't end the interview too abruptly. Take responsibility for the effect on your interviewee if sensitive issues are discussed.

Record, store, and use information safely.

Some 'Do's' for interviews

- Do try to make sure you have a good translator.
- Do locate elders/leaders first, explain who you are and what you are doing, and ask their permission to interview.
- Do ask individuals' permission to interview them; for example, 'Is it OK if I ask you a few questions about the conditions here?' Thank them afterwards.
- Do try to prioritise discussions with women and children, and other people likely to be experiencing particular difficulty.
- Do try and interview at least three families in each location in order to cross-check the information you are receiving.
- Do make sure that you include people at the edge of a camp or site, where you may find the poorest families living, quite literally, on the margins.
- Do avoid large crowds following you around if possible, since this is likely to intimidate interviewees and interviewers.

Source: Schofield (2003)

From: S. Burns and S. Cupitt (2003) 'Managing outcomes: a guide for homelessness organisations', Charities Evaluation Services (adapted); R. Schofield, Medair (internal, adapted). **(ECB Tool 5)**

Tool 13
How to observe

In some situations, informal observation may be all you can do and will be 'good enough' when making an assessment or tracking changes.

'I look to see if people are moving into houses. I ask if they feel safe. Are they smiling? Are they happy? I look to see if children are going back to school.' (John Watt)

Observing people: some tips and possible problems

Tips	Possible problems
Explain why you want to observe people at the site, and how the information you collect will be used. Request permission from the people living there.	Observing people may affect their normal behaviour and routines.
Invite people living there to observe the site with you.	If an observer knows the people being observed well, this may make it hard for him/her to be unbiased.
Give observers brief training and support. Agree the information you want to collect through observation.	Involving many observers can result in many different opinions and interpretations.
Afterwards, compare notes and pool observations as soon as you can. Record your findings in writing and use them.	Findings that are not recorded immediately will be less reliable.

From: *Partners in Evaluation: Evaluating Development and Community Programmes with Participants*, © Marie-Thérèse Feuerstein 1986. Reproduced by permission of Macmillan Publishers Ltd. **(ECB Tool 9)**

Tool 14
How to involve people throughout the project

This tool suggests ways of informing, consulting, involving, and reporting to people affected by an emergency at every stage of the project. It was originally developed for use in villages in Aceh, Indonesia. It can be adapted for other sites too.

Before assessment:

- Determine and clearly state the objectives of the assessment.
- If you can, inform the local community and local authorities well before the assessment takes place.
- Include both women and men in the project team.
- Make a list of vulnerable groups to be identified during the assessment.
- Check what other NGOs have done in that community and get a copy of their reports.

During assessment:

- Introduce team members and their roles.
- Explain the timeframe for assessment.
- Invite representatives of local people to participate.
- Create space for individuals or groups to speak openly.
- Hold separate discussions and interviews with different groups e.g. local officials, community groups, men, women, local staff.
- Ask these groups for their opinions on needs and priorities. Inform them about any decisions taken.
  Note: If it is not possible to consult all groups within the community at one time, state clearly which groups have been omitted and return to meet them as soon as possible. Write up your findings and describe your methodology and its limitations. Use the analysis for future decision-making.

During project design:

- Give local authorities and the community, including the village committee and representatives of affected groups, the findings of the assessment.
- Invite representatives of local people to participate in project design.
- Explain to people their rights as disaster-affected people.

186

- Enable the village committee to take part in project budgeting.
- Check the project design with different groups of beneficiaries.
- Design a complaints and response mechanism.

During project implementation:

- Invite the local community, village committee, and local authorities to take part in developing criteria for selection of beneficiaries.
- Announce the criteria and display them in a public place.
- Invite the local community and village committee to participate in selecting beneficiaries.
- Announce the beneficiaries and post the list in a public place.
- Announce the complaints and response mechanisms and any forum for beneficiaries to raise complaints.

During distribution:

- If recruiting additional staff for distribution, advertise openly e.g. in a newspaper.
- Form a distribution committee comprising the village committee, government official(s), and NGO staff.
- Consider how distribution will include the most vulnerable, such as disabled people, elderly people, and other poor or marginalised groups.
- Give the local authority and local community a date and location for distribution in advance, where safety allows.
- List items for distribution and their cost, and display this list in advance in a public place.
- In order to include people living a long way from the village or distribution point, consider giving them transport costs.
- In order to include vulnerable people, e.g. pregnant women, distribute to them first.
- Ensure that people know how to register complaints.

During monitoring:

- Invite the village committee to take part in the monitoring process.
- Share findings with the village committee and the community.

From: S. Phoeuk (2005) 'Practical Guidelines on Humanitarian Accountability', Oxfam GB Cambodia (internal, adapted). **(ECB Tool 3)**

Tool 15
How to conduct a focus group

If possible, conduct a few focus groups and compare the information you are collecting from these and other sources.

What is a focus group?

Six to twelve people are invited to discuss specific topics in detail. The focus group can bring together people who have something in common. They may share a particular problem, or be unable to speak up at larger meetings (e.g. younger people, women, or minority groups), or are people only peripherally involved in the community, such as nomads. It is best not to have leaders or people in authority present – interview them separately.

Why only six to twelve people?

In a larger group:
- Speaking time will be restricted and dominant people will speak most.
- The facilitator will have to play more of a controlling role.
- Some members of the group will become frustrated if they cannot speak.
- Participants will start talking to one another rather than to the group as a whole.
- The group may stop focusing and start talking about something else.

What do you need?

- An experienced facilitator: a native speaker who can lead, draw out the people who are not talking, and stop others from talking too much.
- Time to prepare open-ended questions and select focus-group members.
- One, sometimes two, people to note in writing what is said.
- A common language.
- A quiet place where the group will not be overheard or interrupted.
- To sit in a circle and be comfortable.
- Shared understanding and agreement about the purpose of the discussion.

188

- Ground rules, e.g. everyone has a right to speak; no one has the right answer; please don't interrupt.
- Permission from the group to take notes (or maybe use a tape recorder).
- About one to one-and-a-half hour's time and some refreshments.

What happens?

- The facilitator makes sure that everyone has a chance to speak and that the discussion stays focused.
- The note-taker writes notes.
- At the end of the session, the facilitator gives a brief summing up of what has been said in case someone has something to add.
- The facilitator checks that the written record has captured the main points and reflected the level of participants' involvement in the discussion.

From: V. M. Walden 'Focus group discussion', Oxfam (internal, adapted); L. Gosling and M. Edwards (2003) 'Toolkits: a practical guide to planning, monitoring, evaluation and impact measurement', Save the Children (adapted); USAID (1996) Performance Monitoring and Evaluation TIPS No. 10, USAID Centre for Development Information and Evaluation (adapted). **(ECB Tool 6)**

Tool 16
How to say goodbye

This tool can help to ensure that your agency's departure at the end of the project is smooth and transparent. The people who have been involved in your project, including beneficiaries, staff, and local partner agencies and authorities, should know what is happening and why.

Define in detail communication needs and activities. These may include:

1. Writing a letter to staff, followed by group and individual meetings.

2. Writing an official letter about project closure for regional, district, and village leaders, including elders and informal leaders. Follow letters with face-to-face briefings. Put a copy of the letter to village leaders on information boards.

3. Using a question and answer sheet to guide staff when communicating with beneficiaries about the end of the project.

4. Planning for the conduct of exit meetings with communities.

5. Reporting on project achievements and learning.

6. Writing a letter to other NGOs and partners. Follow this with face-to-face briefings and meetings.

7. Holding focus groups and/or house-to-house visits to reach women and vulnerable groups who may be unable to attend formal meetings.

8. Using posters and leaflets, including formats appropriate for less literate people.

9. Inviting feedback/comments on project activities.

10. Collecting stories about successful work and positive community interaction. Give these back to the community, e.g. have a photo exhibition during handover.

11. Supporting appropriate cultural activities or celebrations when projects are handed over to the community.

12. Evaluating exit communication activities and recording lessons learned.

From: T. Gorgonio (2006) 'Notes on Accountable Exit from Communities when Programmes Close', Oxfam GB Philippines (internal, adapted). **(ECB Tool 14)**

Tool 17
Heart of community engagement

The elements shown in the diagram, and explained below, together encapsulate informed consent.

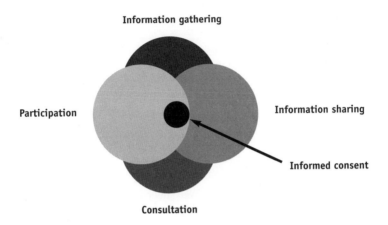

Information gathering

Participation

Information sharing

Informed consent

Consultation

Information gathering: Carry out a needs assessment and interviews.

Information sharing: Explain who you are, what you can and cannot do, and how and when you can carry out services.

Consultation: Discuss what information has been gathered and what options are best.

Participation: Employ various levels of participation throughout the project cycle.

© HAP International

Tool 18
Making a consultation meeting effective

The following questions have been shown to be useful in preparing for a consultation meeting, to ensure that the meeting is effective.

1. What is the aim or purpose of the consultation?
2. What are the issues?
3. Who should be consulted?
4. Whom does the issue affect?
5. Who will manage the consultation? How will the consultation be managed to ensure that all those who need to be consulted (including marginalised groups) are involved?
6. What resources are available for the consultation?
7. What level of commitment, in terms of time and resources, is sought from the community?
8. When would it be best to consult?
9. How much time can be spent?
10. Have similar consultations been carried out by staff before (in this or in other sectors) or are other consultations planned, so that co-ordination can be arranged, information shared, and lessons learned?
11. What information should be prepared and made available in advance to ensure that the community is properly informed?
12. How will the information be used, and by whom?
13. How will the recommendations made by the beneficiaries be implemented?
14 How will the outcomes of the consultation and the final decisions (if applicable) be conveyed to the participants?
15. Where applicable, what role will the community have in the implementation and ongoing management of the project?

Courtesy of World Vision International Tsunami Response Humanitarian Accountability Team based in Sri Lanka, author: Joshua Pepall. © HAP International – tool has been adapted.

Tool 19
Participation strategy framework

A participation strategy framework should consider the following questions:

Question	Comment
1 Have you identified the target community/intended beneficiaries?	This can be done by carrying out a beneficiary mapping exercise, which should identify: • Male/female ratio • Percentage of children, including unaccompanied children • Average household size • Vulnerable groups (e.g. disabled and elderly people) • Traditional/civil structures • Key informants/specified beneficiary representatives • Numbers • A more detailed mapping should reveal what communication methods are appropriate (see Benchmark 2). • Mapping could extend to surveying and capturing the skills and capacities of the beneficiaries (see Benchmark 4).

Question	Comment
2 What type of engagement is possible? Should you engage directly with individual members of the affected population, or via existing structures (local/civil/traditional, etc.)? The latter could result in restricted, or no, access to marginalised groups.	A risk assessment will need to be undertaken to ascertain the consequences of the various engagement options and ensure safety for all involved. Access will play a part, involving cultural and gender dynamics, and physical factors, e.g. the need to ensure that if women beneficiaries cannot talk to male aid workers, then female aid workers are available. Political issues will need to be considered. Engagement possibilities will be affected by the time available – although this should not be used as an excuse not to engage. Trust will affect engagement. Trust takes time to grow, but the process will constantly improve as it is gained.
3 Which approach will work best in the context? **Information approach:** The community is kept informed of what is going to happen (where and when). **Interview approach:** The community is involved through interviews that both deliver information and seek feedback.	A good strategy would use all of these approaches at one time or another, with the aim of moving towards consultation and partnership where possible.

Question	Comment
Consultative approach: Community members are asked for their perspectives. **Employee/volunteer approach:** Community members are asked to contribute through their labour, or are given incentives to participate in other ways. **Partnership approach:** A contractual agreement between the community and the agency outlines responsibilities.	A good strategy would use all of these approaches at one time or another, with the aim of moving towards consultation and partnership where possible.
4 Which tools/methods will work best to: • Map and analyse the community • Interview beneficiaries • Establish selection criteria?	A tool is, among other things, a device/framework/checklist/guideline that provides a mechanical or mental advantage in accomplishing a task.
5 What is the best way to manage the information collected and analysed?	It is important to create a baseline and indicators to help monitor progress and impact. This record is essential for history, accountability, knowledge management, handover, and transparency.

© *HAP International*

Tool 20
Performance assessment checklists

What are competencies?

Competencies ere the application of knowledge, skills, and behaviours in performance. Accountability competencies are competencies which should strengthen cross-cultural communication and thus increase accountability.

Examples of accountability competencies

- Good interpersonal skills
- Cross-cultural experience/gender sensitivity skills
- Language skills
- Self-management skills/disciplines
- Negotiation skills
- Mediation skills
- Diplomatic skills
- Willingness to reflect on and learn from experiences
- Awareness of gender issues in a humanitarian context.

The following is an example of a performance assessment checklist that could be adapted for use by different agencies. It measures the level of competency achieved in each activity.

Activity/skill (linked to job description)	Self-appraisal	Internal appraisal	Training received (date)	Competency achieved (excellent/ good/fair/poor)
1 General Read required agency info (list documents) Read standard operation procedure manual Required knowledge: • codes • standards • laws				
2 Management tasks (skills) (will be particular to the job)				
3 Specific project tasks				
4 Administrative tasks				
5 Communication skills				
6 Security				
7 Etc.				

196

Reasons for poor performance

If performance is still poor after training, you need to learn why. There may be a number of reasons:

- Inadequate training
- Good knowledge and ability, but no resources to carry out expected work: resources could be in the form of time, finances, access, or staff support
- Poor attitude.

Whatever the cause, management action will be required to address it. This can only be done effectively when a quality management system is in place to support the process.

© HAP International

Tool 21
Training tracking record

Training can be defined as a process to provide and develop knowledge, skills, and behaviours to meet with organisational requirements. Training tracking records should be kept as follows:

Sector	Name	Resource person/ organisation	Objective	Curriculum	Number of days (date)	Venue
Health	A. Worker	Health co-ordinator	Under-standing what is in the Essential Drugs List	WHO	2	Project Site – Sudan

© HAP International

198

Tool 22
Complaints mechanisms: tips on file storage and data management

- The electronic complaints register will be backed up monthly onto a CD and stored in a locked filing cabinet.

- The register will be stored on one designated office computer and will be password-protected to keep unauthorised staff from gaining access.

- Confidential hard copies of records must be stored in a filing cabinet in the manager's office with access limited to staff members who are authorised to access it.

- All borrowed records must be issued to the individual who will be using the record, and noted as being located with that person.

- No records or complaints archives are to be loaned to parties outside the organisation.

- Staff members are not permitted to take complaints records outside the office without express permission from the manager.

- In the event of an evacuation, all hard copies are to be destroyed and the hard drive removed from the designated complaints register computer.

- To preserve the integrity of the original complaint information, no additions or alterations of any kind are to be made to any record. This includes purging, adding or removing papers, or annotating papers. If there is a need to record future developments or a change in circumstances, or otherwise reflect inaccurate information or deficiencies, a further document can be generated and attached to the file.

© World Vision

Tool 23
Community feedback system: complaints cards

Introduction

All communities have the basic right to register a protest regarding unfair treatment, report cases of wrongdoing, and seek fulfillment of their rights. A system which enables this to happen is a challenge to implement in an initial relief response, but nevertheless a system should be established in the first 90 days. Receiving complaints and responding to them is central to accountability, impact, and learning. It is also a formal recognition of the power imbalance between beneficiaries and agencies. Social justice begins to be addressed when these power imbalances are addressed.

A good community complaints mechanism will serve several ends. First, it assists with transparency by creating a channel for people to register concerns. Second, it provides a mechanism for people to report corruption and the abuse of power by the organisation or staff, e.g. the exploitation of vulnerable groups such as children or unaccompanied women. Third, it provides unique and invaluable sources of information to be used for better project management and outcomes.

When it comes to setting up a community complaints system it is worthwhile remembering that there is no 'one size fits all' approach. The system needs to take into consideration, and be responsive to, language, literacy, numeracy, and the needs of women, children, and people with disabilities. Community members need to be consulted and involved in development of the system. Beneficiaries may not themselves use 'relief jargon', but indigenous accountability systems are there. The cards contained in this tool are designed to help humanitarian workers identify and include the community in the complaints system.

Picture cards are engaging and can make complex ideas digestible and easy to work with. They can also be used as prompts for staff unfamiliar with the topic. In Sri Lanka, field staff initially reluctant to use a complaints system were won over to the idea because the cards helped them to structure the community meeting. They felt confident, and as a result the community engaged more fully with the process.

The cards can be used with Tool 24 (ECB Tool 12) and are a grass-roots, accountability action learning tool that focuses participants' attention, facilitates their input, and assists in the:

- identification of existing indigenous complaints systems
- rights of beneficiaries and others to file a complaint
- purpose, parameters, and limitations of the complaints system
- procedure for submitting complaints
- steps taken in processing complaints and the complaints that the agency can and cannot handle
- formation of a confidentiality and non-retaliation policy for complainants
- development of a referral system for complaints that the agency is not equipped to handle
- response, i.e. the right of the beneficiary to receive a response to the complaint.

Poorer and illiterate people who are often excluded can be included by the use of the tool and a group process to facilitate greater participation. Consulting and involving stakeholders in the development of the complaints mechanism helps also to generate a sense of ownership: people are more likely to use a system that they have been involved in developing.

Complaints cards

A field kit should be put together which includes:

- 11 picture cards
- 10 arrows
- paper and pens.

The cards and arrows are reproduced at the end of this tool. They are also available on the accompanying CD-ROM (where they are in colour). You can photocopy them from the book or print them from the CD, increasing or decreasing the size to suit your purposes. Laminate the cards and arrows, and cut them out. Do make your own cards if necessary, but always check with local staff to make sure they will not be misunderstood.

The cards represent the following things:

- letter
- community notice board
- community log book
- complaints form
- question
- questions box
- phone
- World Vision/agency
- children
- disabilities
- women

There is a danger that women, children, and people with disabilities can be left out of discussions because of stigma. Use the women, children, and disabilities cards to raise the issue of accessibility with small groups and with these people themselves. For example, a wheelchair user may not be able to access a community notice board if it is on a hill or at the top of steps. Alternatively, the complaints form card could be used to draw attention to an unsuitable height or location.

How to use the cards

1. The cards work best in small groups. If you are using them in a community meeting, split people into groups of up to ten people. Run separate workshops for men, women, and children if required.

2. Quickly review the aim and purpose of the meeting, i.e. to provide information on community complaints mechanisms, answer questions, and discuss how stakeholders can be involved in the development of a complaints mechanism. Emphasise that you are there to learn from people and to come up with a system relevant to their needs. Answer any questions about the process before you move on. If people have specific complaints, ask them to wait until the end of the workshop and allow some time to answer their questions. This time is an investment in the future of the complaints systems, so don't rush off. Try to

find a solution as soon as possible and refer people to other agencies if needed. People will be watching to see if you take these initial complaints seriously.

3. If the agency is present as part of an emergency response, people may not know who it is, or who you are. Explain your organisation's mandate, its areas of work, and other relevant information. See Tool 10 for further information.

4. Work through the cards explaining what each one means. Pass them around the group.

5. When you have finished, lay the cards out on the ground or table. Work your way through the following points:

   - Brainstorm any existing complaints systems and how local people use them. Make a list. Ask what is good about each system and what isn't.
   - Place your agency's card in the middle of the floor or table. Explain why you want to set up a complaints system.
   - Ask group members to choose a card with which to make a complaint or ask a question about the programme. Use an arrow to indicate how each complaint card leads to the next. For instance, if people want to make a complaint by making a phone call to the office, use the arrow to point to the community notice board, where the phone numbers of staff can be placed. This would lead to a discussion of where the community notice board should be situated and, using the children, women, and disability cards, a discussion about accessibility; you could raise the cost of making a call and ask whether the poorest people in the community have access to a phone. One card will flow to the next. See next page for an example of what your 'map' might look like.
   - Draw the map for later reference. A copy will need to be distributed to the community and can be displayed on the community notice board.
   - When people are satisfied with the map, discuss the following points:
     - Confidentiality and non-retaliation policy for complainants
     - Your agency's child-protection policy
     - Those complaints that you can and cannot handle
     - A referral system for complaints that you cannot handle

- A complaints form
- Monitoring mechanisms to ensure that the system is working.

6. Be adaptable and creative. If you need to add another picture card not included in the kit, ask a participant to select a stone, rock, twig, or something readily available and use that.

7. At the end of the session, thank people for their participation, provide your office contact details, answer outstanding participant questions, and address any misconceptions.

8. Using the community complaints map, provide feedback to staff and the community once the system has been set up.

© World Vision / Joshua Pepall (Humanitarian Accountability Advisor) World Vision Sri Lanka – tool has been adapted.

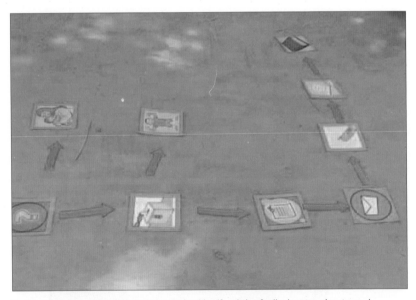

The Community Complaints Cards are being used to identify existing feedback systems in a tsunami community in order to design a project feedback and complaints system. (Sri Lanka)
© Haig Bailan/World Vision 2007

2.

3.

8.

World Vision®

1. Humanitarian Accountability Team-World Vision LTRT Sri Lanka–Developed By Joshua Pepall

7.

11.

4.

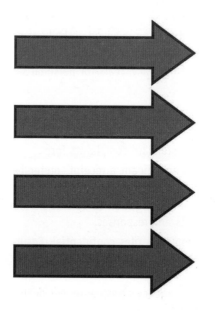

210

Tool 24
How to set up a complaints and response mechanism

Feedback can be positive or negative: complaints mean that things may have gone wrong. Receiving complaints and responding to them is central to accountability, impact, and learning.

Information

Tell people how to complain and that it is their right to do so.

- Use staff and notice boards to give information about complaints processes.
- Be clear about the types of complaint you can and cannot deal with.
- Know your agency's procedures on abuse or exploitation of beneficiaries.
- Explain details of the appeals process.

Accessibility

Make access to the complaints process as easy and safe as possible. Consider:

- How will beneficiaries in remote locations be able to make complaints?
- Can complaints be received verbally or only in writing?
- Is it possible to file a complaint on behalf of somebody else (owing to illiteracy, fears for personal safety, inability to travel, etc.)?

Procedures

Describe how complaints will be handled.

- Develop a standard complaints form.
- Give the complainant a receipt, preferably a copy of their signed form.
- Enable an investigation to be tracked and keep statistics on complaints and responses.
- Keep complaints files confidential. Ensure that discussion about the complaint cannot be traced back to the individual complainant.
- Know your agency's procedures for dealing with complaints against staff.

Response

Give beneficiaries a response to their complaint.

- Make sure that each complainant receives a response and appropriate action.
- Be consistent: ensure that similar complaints receive a similar response.
- Maintain oversight of complaints processes and have an appeals process.

Learning

Learn from complaints and mistakes.

- Collect statistics and track any trends.
- Feed learning into decision-making and project activities.

A complaints and response mechanism in action

Medair responded to the Kashmir earthquake in October 2005 with emergency shelter and non-food items. The team soon realised that it needed a mechanism to address constant queries and complaints. One hour a day was dedicated to dealing with complaints at the main project base. This was the only time that Medair would receive complaints.

A complainant could speak to the administrator or office manager. If possible, complaints were resolved informally. Otherwise, office staff completed a complaints form and passed this to an assessment team in the field. Complaints about staff members were investigated by the project manager at each base.

Most complaints came from earthquake survivors who had not received a shelter. They also came from people outside Medair's own project area. In those cases, Medair lobbied the responsible agency. Sometimes, if nothing happened, Medair provided help itself. If a complaint investigated by an assessment team was upheld, the beneficiary received assistance, depending on Medair's resources.

A spreadsheet recorded the numbers of complaints from each village, and how many complaints had been dealt with. This enabled project staff to assess progress and to integrate complaints into project planning.

By the end of the emergency phase, Medair had dealt with approximately 1,600 complaints, 70 per cent of all those it had received. Not all complaints could be investigated because by March 2006 Medair had used up its project funds. Checking more households would raise false expectations. Also, five months after the earthquake, most homes had been rehabilitated. Of the complaints investigated, 18 per cent were upheld. Complaints about staff led to dismissal for three individuals who had given preferential treatment to their tribal or family members.

The complaints mechanism saved Medair teams significant time in both field and office and in identifying gaps in coverage. By using this mechanism, Medair helped 290 families whose needs would otherwise have been overlooked.

Medair was new to Pakistan and the complaints and response mechanism helped to compensate for limited local knowledge. By the end of the project, communities would contact Medair about any discrepancy they saw in its distributions, confident that the agency would take appropriate action.

From: written communication with Robert Schofield and John Primrose, Medair (adapted). **(ECB Tool 12)**

Tool 25
Notes and guidelines about complaints-handling

1. Identify what has gone wrong

In order to help the complaints mechanism work effectively and efficiently, clarification may be needed to identify exactly what went wrong. Help the complainant(s) to clarify exactly what they are dissatisfied with, as this will aid a prompt response process. Some prompts to help clarify the situation include:

- Was it the way you were treated?
- Was it a decision that was taken?
- Were the items distributed defective?
- Can you define exactly what went wrong?

ACTION: Draft a complaints form that helps to categorise the type and cause of the complaint.

2. Determine what outcome or solution the complainant expects

Asking the complainant to suggest a corrective action is a constructive way of rebuilding relationships and acknowledging your willingness to hear their point of view. For example:

- Do they want replacement of defective items distributed?
- Do they want recognition of poor treatment and an apology?
- Does an investigation need to be started?
- What would they recommend as a way to avoid this happening in the future?

ACTION: Ensure that a section of the complaints form helps the complainant to think through what solution they would like to see occur.

3. Be creative in developing complaints-submissions procedures

Methods used in recent emergencies include mobile phones, complaints boxes, village 'complaints and compliments' books, tape recorders, verbal communication to accountability monitors, letters, group complaints, and many more.

ACTION: Ask national staff and community members what would be appropriate ways for people to submit complaints. Ensure that vulnerable groups are not excluded.

4. Explain clearly how a complaint can be lodged and how it will be processed

A 'complaints procedures guide' that contains a full explanation of how the system works will enable the complainant to follow the process properly and understand what service they can expect. See requirement 5.2 under Benchmark 5 in the HAP Standard for full guidance on what should be contained in the complaints procedures guide. To further underline the agency's commitment to respond to complaints, a senior authority contact should also be given. This could be someone within the agency or a specified independent body, such as HAP.

ACTION: After developing the complaints procedures guide, decide on the appropriate way to disseminate the guidelines and contact details.

5. Information systems and complaints mechanisms are closely linked

Usually it is a lack of information which leads to a complaint. For example, people are unclear of the beneficiary criteria, or distribution plan, or quality/quantity of goods, or expected standards of staff behaviour, etc. Experience suggests that improvements in the quality and relevance of information dissemination results in a proportional reduction of complaints received. Further, many complaints received will be relevant to many people, and so can be answered publicly through the agency's information mechanism. Information and complaints mechanisms are closely linked.

ACTION: Good quality information systems (see Benchmark 2) should be developed alongside complaints-handling procedures.

6. Complaints data should be used to improve programme performance

In commercial sectors, complaints data are often seen as a source of valuable information from clients. Companies use complaints information to change product designs and marketing processes. Although the contexts are different, most complainants are similar in that they tend to feel very strongly about an issue, and then think very carefully before making the effort to communicate their concerns and grievances. This information carries weight and legitimacy.

The data resulting from complaints are useful to inform the agency about the:

- impact of its work
- satisfaction of beneficiaries

- potential problems
- possible security issues.

Complaints data contribute to other ongoing monitoring and impact measurement systems.

ACTION: Maintain complaints data by simply recording the number and type of complaints which come in, as well as the corrective actions taken. Complaints data should be regularly analysed by management staff.

7. Complaints-handling systems need to be designed to handle extreme cases of abuse

Although they are more rare, extremely sensitive complaints about fraud, theft, violence, intimidation, and sexual abuse need to be handled by the agency. The complaints procedures guidelines need to provide clear assurances that sensitive complaints can be submitted through different channels (e.g. straight to the director or to a nominated person in the agency/clinic etc.), and that they will be treated separately. In the case of allegations of illegal activities, agencies may need to take legal advice, and in many cases may need to launch an investigation, which may make the complainant reluctant to be exposed.

ACTION: Ensure that your system has various channels for submitting complaints and ensure that confidentiality can be strictly maintained. Take advice from the Building Safer Organisations Project, or from other specialist bodies dealing with extreme cases of abuse.

8. Joint complaints-handling procedures can be more cost-effective and efficient

Complaints-handling mechanisms require resources to set them up and maintain them. However, the benefits of investing are certainly returned in terms of increased efficiency, better relations, increased trust, and more. Joining forces with other agencies can reduce costs, and can also raise the level of mutual transparency and trust to new levels.

ACTION: Consider developing joint mechanisms with other agencies, especially HAP members, on the basis that there will be cost savings, improved performance, better relationships, better security, and other benefits.

© HAP International

Tool 26
Points to remember when implementing a complaints-handling mechanism

	Key point	Comment
1	People should know about the procedure and have easy physical access to use it.	An awareness campaign should be carried out and information regarding how the mechanism works should be made easily available on an ongoing basis.
2	The procedure itself should be non-threatening to use and even welcoming, to actively solicit feedback and complaints.	Fear and ignorance will be the most important issues to overcome. Just because you don't receive complaints doesn't mean there aren't any.
3	There should be limits to the type of complaints solicited. Complaints should only be encouraged about activities and functions for which the agency is claiming responsibility.	An agency can only deal with complaints that are within its realm of authority. If complaints are submitted that the agency cannot deal with, the system should notify the complainant why this is the case.
4	The recording and transmission of complaints information should ensure that a complaint is clearly understood and transmitted without any alteration.	In cases where a verbal complaint is being transcribed by a second person, or when a written complaint is being translated, there is scope for misrepresentation. Staff who are handling complaints need to be trained and monitored.
5	Complainants should be given tangible acknowledge-ment that the complaint has been received.	Use either a number/note or some other appropriate acknowledgement mechanism.
6	Complainants should receive an answer within a stated period.	This time period should be realistic and established prior to set-up.

	Key point	Comment
7	All complaints should be dealt with sensitively and confidentially.	The safety and protection of both those submitting complaints and those handling them are paramount.
8	The complainant should receive a response that comprises a clear answer and explanation, as well as an indication that the complaint has gone through an established due process.	People need to know that they have been heard and answered. This will build trust between the agency and beneficiaries.
9	The complainant should acknowledge that they have understood the answer, and know that if they do not accept it they can complain again.	The mechanism should have an appeal/referral system that users are able to access and follow up.
10	Complainants and staff should be made aware that the system has alternative channels for grievance, and these should be explained.	This may be best presented in a flowchart.
11	No complaint should be ignored.	Ignoring complaints will reduce trust in the system and agency.

© HAP International

Tool 27
Step-by-step guide to setting up a complaints-handling mechanism

Step 1: Build staff awareness of and commitment to complaints-handling

Staff commitment to manage and use a complaints-handling procedure is a critical factor for success. Team discussions and awareness-raising materials can be used to build staff understanding and appreciation of the importance of complaints. Issues to highlight to staff include the right of beneficiaries to complain; benefits and challenges of handling complaints; and organisational commitment to handle complaints. Staff can also be a good source of knowledge about what complaints procedures could be appropriate in the context. Staff could also be asked to anticipate the most common types of complaints and then consider whether an information campaign could pre-empt and reduce these.

Step 2: Develop appropriate complaint submission mechanisms

Beneficiaries need to be able to submit complaints in ways that suit them. Women, men, children, elderly people, people with disabilities, and those who are illiterate all need to be able to submit complaints with relative ease and confidence. Alternative mechanisms may need to be considered depending on the nature of the complaint or the status of the complainant (e.g. serious allegations of abuse may need to go straight to the project director).

Before consulting beneficiaries, agency staff should agree the local language terminology to be used and consider any context-specific sensitivities (e.g. when consulting communities where one person expects to be the representative, or when working in areas where security forces may be suspicious of encouraging a complaints procedure). During the consultation process, beneficiaries and their representatives should be provided with clear information regarding the purpose and rationale for a complaints-handling procedure.

Step 3: Develop a complaints-handling procedure

A complaints-handling procedure needs to be clear and documented. The integrity of the system is essential to its success. If staff or beneficiaries believe that the stated procedure is not followed, then the system as a whole can lose legitimacy. The procedure can be simple but it must be realistic, so that it is feasible to follow. It should contain at least the following basic information:

- Statement of 'purpose' and 'organisational commitment' to handling complaints from beneficiaries.

- Statement of 'parameters', to explain that only complaints about activities or decisions within the control of the agency can be handled.

- Statement of 'referral', to explain what will be done with complaints received that fall outside of the agency's control.

- Statement of 'confidentiality', wherever requested by complainant.

- Explanation of mechanism for submission of complaints.

- Explanation of steps that will be taken to process complaints received.

The procedures should be developed with significant input from both the project team and from beneficiaries.

Step 4: Disseminate the complaints-handling procedure

It is vital that beneficiaries and staff can access and understand the complaints-handling procedure. Use different media and/or simplified texts to increase reach. A strategic dissemination of the procedure, e.g. rolling it out at one project site at a time, may help to slowly build up agency capacity to handle complaints, and allow for the procedure to be tested.

Step 5: Process all complaints according to the documented procedures

A complaints-handling procedure will become legitimate and trusted only if the procedure is seen to be followed strictly. Check regularly that complaints submitted are being processed properly.

Step 6: Make use of the complaints data

Complaints data should be used to inform programme management and to guide or revise the general information provided to beneficiaries. Information systems for beneficiaries and complaints mechanisms are linked, as often it is a lack of information that leads to a complaint.

© *HAP International*

Tool 28
Corrective and preventative action plan tracking guide

An example of how to manage the numerous actions identified that will improve both the accountability framework and the quality management system:

Ref. no.	Finding	Origin	Action	Person	Time	Resources	Priority/ impact

Explanation for headings

Reference number: Discussing entries will be easier if each entry is given a unique reference number. Classification could be taken one step further by noting whether the entry is:
- corrective or
- preventative.

Tracking this trend is helpful for managers, because if all entries are corrective it would appear that management is mainly firefighting (reactive). With time, the number of corrective entries should decrease and the number of preventative actions should increase, signalling more proactive management.

Finding: A very brief description of the problem.

Origin: It is useful to track the origin of the finding, as it will indicate what mechanisms are helping to identify areas of improvement. It may also indicate the need to improve processes that do not work.

For example, if all entries come from external evaluation or audits, there should be concern as to why internal monitoring and evaluation systems are not picking up these findings.

Proposals for improvements can come from all stakeholder groups.

Action: A brief description of the resolution/action required to remedy the finding, to ensure improvement.

To support the monitoring of the implementation of the action, it may be helpful to draft a few key indicators that will help to determine whether the action has solved the problem.

Person: It is always good practice to appoint one person to oversee the implementation, even though many staff may be involved. This person is the focal point and will be responsible for ensuring that the actions are carried out in a timely fashion.

Time: A clear and realistic timeframe to implement the improvement is necessary. One step further would be to indicate interim monitoring dates to ensure that progress is on target.

Resources: To complete the improvement process, adequate resources will be needed, whether in funding, staff time, or materials. These should be quantified.

Priority/impact: As there will inevitably be a number of pressing improvement proposals, it is recommended that a guide is given on how to prioritise. One way is of doing this is to consider the impact of not applying the improvement process versus applying it. Where the consequence of doing nothing would be serious concerns for the well-being of beneficiaries or staff, the improvements would have a higher priority than other proposals.

© *World Vision*

Tool 29
How to hold a lessons-learned meeting

Purpose
- For project staff to meet and to share project information
- To build agreement on the activities you are carrying out
- To build agreement on the changes you aim to make
- To document key information and decisions and act on them.

You will need
- Your accountability adviser, if you have one
- One person to act as facilitator
- Another person to record in writing key findings, comments, and decisions.

Questions for project staff
1. Which people are you working with?
2. Which of these people are particularly vulnerable?
3. Who have you spoken to since the last meeting?
4. What have you learned from them?
5. Who have you cross-referenced findings with?
6. How do findings compare with your meeting records and/or baseline data?
7. What needs are beneficiaries prioritising?
8. How does this relate to your current activities?
9. What is working well?
10. What is not working well?
11. What results are you achieving/should you aim to achieve, and how?
12. What do you need to do to improve impact?

When meetings are held regularly, with key findings, comments, decisions, and dates noted, this can help you update project information and measure project impact. It is particularly important to try to do this during the early stages when you are busy responding, when staff turnover may be high, and when teams have little time to set up systems.

From: written communication with Pauline Wilson and staff at World Vision International (adapted). **(ECB Tool 11)**

Annex 4: Quality and accountability initiatives

The heightened interest in quality and accountability in humanitarian action has stimulated a wide range of initiatives over the past 15 years, aimed at tackling the issue from a variety of angles. These initiatives share the common goal of improving accountability, quality, and performance within the humanitarian sector, but each has a distinctive path and approach, often addressing a particular facet of this complex area. Participants in several of these initiatives meet on a regular basis to co-ordinate their work, and in 2007 a group of them articulated a shared vision on quality and accountability, setting out their common analysis, while affirming the complementarity of each approach.

A shared vision on quality and accountability (Q & A)

People affected by disasters have limited options and little power over their access to assistance and protection. Humanitarian organisations therefore have an ethical responsibility to respect the dignity of victims and to do their utmost to ensure that their assistance programmes are of the best possible quality.

Humanitarian agencies should respond meaningfully to needs, take into consideration local capacities and constraints, and respect and involve crisis-affected people. Any response should avoid or mitigate negative impacts while fostering positive effects.

Organisations have to manage and support their staff members well; they should evaluate and learn from experience, and use resources efficiently and transparently. Organisations should be able to demonstrate commitment to improving their performance through verification and reporting systems.

The different Q & A initiatives are collaborating around this shared vision, through identifying possible synergies, and clarifying their differences, in order to offer a collective palette of choices. Humanitarian organisations can then select the options best suited to their needs and priorities. The six initiatives* currently participating in the Q&A initiative are committed to working together to facilitate this process of selection, and to reporting progress to the larger humanitarian constituency.

* The six initiatives are ALNAP, Coordination Sud, Groupe URD, HAP, People In Aid, and The Sphere Project.

Many agencies interested in the HAP Standard will also have subscribed to other standards and will be collaborating with a wide range of agencies and projects. The HAP certification system understands and welcomes this cross-fertilisation and encourages agencies to include other standards, codes, and principles in their humanitarian accountability framework. A list of some of the main initiatives is given here, with accompanying web links. Further information is also available in The Guide to the HAP Standard supplementary material posted on the HAP website (www.hap international.org). A list of key legal instruments and related web links is also provided below.

Links to quality initiatives

Initiative	Link
AccountAbility	www.accountability21.net
ACFID: Code of Conduct	www.acfid.asn.au/code-of-conduct
ALNAP	www.alnap.org/
ALPS	www.actionaid.org/assets/pdf/ ALPS2006FINAL_14FEB06.pdf
Building Safer Organisations Project	ww.icva.ch/doc00000706.html
Do No Harm Project	www.cdainc.com/dnh/about_dnh.php
ECB: Emergency Capacity Building Project	www.ecbproject.org/
Good Humanitarian Donorship Principles	www.goodhumanitariandonorship.org/
InterAction PVO Standard	www.interaction.org/pvostandards/index.html
InterAction: NGO Field Cooperation Protocol	http://interaction.org/disaster/NGO_field.html
International NGOs Accountability Charter	www.amnesty.org/en/who-we-are/accountability/ ingo-charter
MANGO	www.mango.org.uk/guide/resources.aspx
One World Trust: GAP	www.oneworldtrust.org/accountability
People In Aid	www.peopleinaid.org
Quality COMPAS	www.projetqualite.org/en/index/index.php
Red Cross/Red Crescent Code of Conduct	www.ifrc.org/publicat/conduct/index.asp
Social Accountability International	www.sa-intl.org/
The Sphere Project	www.sphereproject.org/
Synergie Qualité	www.coordinationsud.org/
Transparency International	www.transparency.org/tools

Links to selected legal instruments

Instrument	Link
Convention on the Rights of the Child: 1989	www.unicef.org/crc/
Convention Relating to the Status of Refugees: 1951	www.unhchr.ch/html/menu3/b/o_c_ref.htm
Convention against Torture and other Cruel, Inhuman or Degrading Treatment or Punishment: 1984	www.unhchr.ch/html/menu3/b/h_cat39.htm
Convention on the Prevention and Punishment of the Crime of Genocide: 1948	www.unhchr.ch/html/menu3/b/p_genoci.htm
Convention on the Elimination of All Forms of Discrimination against Women: 1979	www.unhchr.ch/html/menu3/b/e1cedaw.htm
Convention relating to the Status of Stateless Persons: 1960	www2.ohchr.org/english/law/stateless.htm
Geneva Conventions	www.icrc.org/Web/Eng/siteeng0.nsf/htmlall/genevaconventions?opendocument
Guiding Principles on Internal Displacement: 1998	www.unhchr.ch/html/menu2/7/b/principles.htm
International Covenant on Civil and Political Rights: 1966	www.unhchr.ch/html/menu3/b/a_ccpr.htm
International Covenant on Economic, Social and Cultural Rights: 1966	www.unhchr.ch/html/menu3/b/a_cescr.htm
International Convention on the Elimination of All Forms of Racial Discrimination: 1969	www.ohchr.org/english/law/cerd.htm
Universal Declaration of Human Rights: 1948	www.unhchr.ch/udhr/index.htm

Annex 5: Acknowledgements

The drafting of the HAP Humanitarian Accountability and Quality Management Standard (2007) and of the subsequent Guide to the HAP Standard have drawn on a wide and diverse group of stakeholders, all committed to promoting and strengthening accountability to people affected by disaster. Each step in the development of the HAP Standard followed internationally recognised principles.

The principles for creating the Standard are:

1. **Consensus: the views of all those interested should be taken into account.** In July 2005, HAP invited identified stakeholders to participate in the consultation and development of the Standard and its Guide. Some 232 individuals joined the Standard Development Reference Group. This group was made up of 45 different nationalities and included eight disaster survivors, staff from 122 organisations (including seven UN agencies), ten donors, and 12 quality initiatives.

2. **Sector-wide: the Standard should seek international/global solutions for humanitarian accountability and quality management.** Although HAP was mandated to create the Standard initially for its own members, it was recognised that there was a need for such a standard for the humanitarian sector as a whole – hence the

consultations, workshops, and reference group input from the wider sector. Information regarding each stage of the development process was regularly posted on the HAP website and sent to the Reference Group.

3. **Voluntary: involvement at all stages of development of the Standard should be voluntary.** Participation in the HAP Standard development project was entirely voluntary.

Structure of the consultation process

Management of the Standard development process was undertaken by the **Editorial Steering Committee**, which was divided into two sections:

Management team
Standards Development Manager and Co-author: Sheryl Haw
HAP Executive Director and Co-author: Nicholas Stockton
HAP Programme Advisor: Zia Choudhury
HAP Researcher: Jennifer Birdsall
HAP Communications Manager: Andrew Lawday
Contributor: Asmita Naik

Advisory team
Drawn from HAP staff, HAP members, disaster survivors, and quality initiatives:

Alex Jacobs – MANGO
Dr. Chol Obuongo – disaster survivor, South Sudan
Jock Baker – CARE International
Alison Joyner – The Sphere Project
Dr. Majed Nassar – disaster survivor, Palestine
Mamadou Ndiaye – OFADEC
Amineh Starvidis – disaster survivor, Palestine
Dr. Salim Bahramand – disaster survivor, Afghanistan
Marcus Oxley – Tearfund UK
Basil Lucima – HAP Sudan

Dr. Yasamin Yousofzai – disaster survivor, Afghanistan
Nelly Badaru – disaster survivor, Uganda
Branka Mraovic – disaster survivor, Serbia
Elena Tiffert-Vaughan – Medical Aid for Palestinians
Peter Klansoe – Danish Refugee Council
Clare Smith – CARE International
Emmanuel Minari – HAP
Robert Schofield – Medair
David Bainbridge – Tearfund UK
Ivan Scott – Oxfam GB
Ton van Zutphen – World Vision International

HAP members

HAP members provided feedback and platforms for trials and field tests of the Standard, hosting workshops and carrying out self-assessments. Several members provided examples of good practice and, in some cases, tools that are included in the Guide.

Full members

The Australian Council for International Development (ACFID); CAFOD; CARE International; Christian Aid; Concern Worldwide, DanChurchAid (DCA); Danish Refugee Council (DRC); Medical Aid for Palestinians (MAP); Medair; MERCY Malaysia; Norwegian Refugee Council (NRC); OFADEC; Oxfam GB; Save the Children UK; Tearfund UK; Women's Commission for Refugee Women and Children (WCRWC); World Vision International (WVI).

Associate members

DANIDA; DFID; MANGO; SIDA.

Quality initiatives

HAP has tried to involve all interested stakeholders and, in particular, has recognised the importance of drawing on the expertise and insight of many quality and accountability initiatives, including: ECB; The Sphere Project, People In Aid; MANGO; Transparency International; ALNAP; One World Trust; Group URD; SCHR; GlobalScale; Social Accountability International; AccountAbility.

Donors

AusAID/ACFID; DFID; IrishAid; DANIDA; SIDA; Netherlands MFA; Ford Foundation; SDC; Oxfam GB; ECB; World Vision International.

Reference Group

The Reference Group was drawn from a wide and diverse group of individuals, based in the following organisations:

Agency Coordinating Body for Afghan Relief	Ausaid	CARE UK
AccountAbility	Beyond Borders	CARE USA
Action Contre la Faim	Bioforce	Caritas Australia
Action Aid	British Red Cross	Channel Research
Adventist Development & Relief Agency	BushProof	Christian Aid
The Australian Council for International Development	CAFOD	Christian Children's Fund
	CARE Australia	Colombia University
	CARE Bangladesh	Concern
Aid World ICT	CARE Cambodia	Concern Cambodia
Al Manar	CARE Indonesia	Development Cooperation Ireland
ALNAP	CARE International	DfID/CHASE
American Red Cross	CARE Kenya	Danish Refugee Care
American Refugee Care	CARE Laos	DRC Serbia
Amnesty International	CARE Philippines	D-Trac
	CARE Sierra Leone	

ECHO SE Asia

ECHO Sri Lanka

Emergency Capacity Building Project

Emma Ltd

Ethical Globalization Initiative

EU-CORD

FHI Mozambique

Ford Foundation

Glemminge

Global Scale

Graduate Institute of International & Development Studies

Group URD

Handicap International

HAP International

HelpAge International

Humanitarian Policy Group – ODI

Humanitarian Times

Inter Agency Standing Committee

International Aid Services

International Council for Voluntary Agencies

International Federation of Red Cross and Red Crescent Societies

International Institute for Humanitarian Law

InterAction

The International Peacebuilding Alliance

Irish Aid

IRC Kenya

Islamic Relief

MANGO

Medical Aid for Palestinians

Medair

Ministry of Foreign Affairs

Norwegian Refugee Council

OFADEC

One World Trust

OSCE Parliamentary Assembly

Oxfam Bangladesh

Oxfam DRC

Oxfam GB

Oxfam East Asia (Thailand)

Oxfam Indonesia

Oxfam Liberia

Oxfam Solidarité Belgique

Oxfam South Africa

Oxfam Sri Lanka

Oxfam USA

Oxfam Viet Nam

People In Aid

Save the Children UK

SCF UK Senegal

SCF UK Sri Lanka

Steering Committee for Humanitarian Response

Swiss Development Cooperation

Serbian Refugee Council

Shelter Centre

SIDA

The Sphere Project

Swiss Peace

Tearfund UK

Terre des Hommes

The Leprosy Mission

Transparency International

Tufts University

UN-UNICEF/EMOPS

UN-WFP

UN-WHO

VBNK

VIVA

Voluntary Organisations in Cooperation in Emergencies

Women's Commission for Refugee Women and Children

World Bank

World Council of Churches

World Relief

World Vision Cambodia

World Vision Colombia

World Vision International

World Vision Kenya

World Vision South Africa

World Vision Sri Lanka

World Vision USA

ZOA

Thanks

HAP would like to thank everyone who participated in the drafting of the Standard and Guide. It has been both an inspiring and a humbling process, in which we recognise how much insight has been gained, how much progress has been made, and how much good work has been and is being done around the world in humanitarian aid provision. The resulting Standard and Guide are really yours, as they represent what we together have identified as mission-critical to ensuring that we have a humanitarian system that champions the rights and dignity of people affected by disaster. We believe that compliance with the HAP Standard will ensure a humanitarian sector with a trusted, transparent, and accessible accountability framework that is relevant and meaningful for all.

We would have liked to mention each person and agency who participated in drafting the Standard by name here, but recognise that the list would take up many pages, so we have therefore provided a full list on the HAP website: www.hapinternational.org/ and accompanying CD-ROM.

Index

The full text of the HAP Standard appears in Annex 1. Much of this same text appears throughout the rest of the book, where there are guidelines on how to *use* the Standard. Where indexed terms appear in both places in the text, both page references will be given. Page references in italics followed by *A, t,* and *b* refer to Annex entries, tables, and boxes respectively.